Castration and Male Rage

Marie-Louise von Franz, Honorary Patron

**Studies in Jungian Psychology
by Jungian Analysts**

Daryl Sharp, General Editor

CASTRATION AND MALE RAGE

The Phallic Wound

Eugene Monick

Also by Eugene Monick in this series:
Phallos: Sacred Image of the Masculine (title 27, 1987)

Canadian Cataloguing in Publication Data

Monick, Eugene
    Castration and male rage

(Studies in Jungian psychology by Jungian analysts; 50)

Includes bibliographical references and index.

ISBN 0-919123-51-1

1. Castration—Psychological aspects.
2. Penis—Psychological aspects.
3. Masculinity (Psychology).
4. Men—Psychology.
5. Jung, C.G. (Carl Gustav), 1875-1961.
I. Title. II. Series.

BF692.5.M66 1991   155.3'32   C90-095913-4

Copyright © 1991 by Eugene Monick.
All rights reserved.

INNER CITY BOOKS
Box 1271, Station Q, Toronto, Canada M4T 2P4
Telephone (416) 927-0355
FAX 416-924-1814

Honorary Patron: Marie-Louise von Franz.
Publisher and General Editor: Daryl Sharp.
Senior Editor: Victoria Cowan.

INNER CITY BOOKS was founded in 1980 to promote the understanding and practical application of the work of C.G. Jung.

Cover: Henri Matisse, *La Musique* (detail), 1910.
    (Musée de l'Ermitage, Leningrad)

Index by Daryl Sharp

Printed and bound in Canada by
University of Toronto Press Incorporated

Contents

Introduction 9

1 **Masculinity and Transformation** 16
The Masculine Grid 20
Six Stages of Masculine Transformation 23
   Prenatal 24
   Pre-oedipal 25
   Oedipal 28
   Adolescent 29
   Accomplishment 30
   Individuation 32

2 **Castration in Freud, Jung and Others** 39
Sigmund Freud 39
   Libido and phallos 40
   The oedipal conflict 41
   Summary of castration in Freud's thinking 47
   The castration complex 49
   Two Freudians: Karen Horney and Heinz Kohut 50
C.G. Jung 55
   The hero 57
   Wotan and individuation 59
   What does it mean to integrate the feminine? 66

3 **Castration and Male Rage** 78
Male-Male Castration 79
Female-Male Castration 83
Auto-Castration 86
Societal Castration 89
Castration by Fate 93
Ontological Castration 96
Rage 98
The Paradox of Castration 104

4 Coming to Terms with Castration 108
Signs of Castration 108
Antidotes to Castration 112
   Mentoring 112
   Touching 114
   Collegiality 117
   Sadness 119
   Respect 121
   Deconstruction 123

5 Epilogue: Masthead Reborn 126

Bibliography 136

Index 139

See last page for descriptions of other Inner City Books

My work will be continued by those who suffer.
—C.G. Jung, *The Wisdom of the Heart.*

Phallic stone in Jung's garden at Bollingen. The Greek inscription, carved by Jung, reads: "To the most beautiful Attis." (see text, pp. 86-87; photo by Monick)

Introduction

Why are men so angry? What is it about men that so often places them on the cusp of hatred? How can men, long at the top of our cultural pyramid of power, be infantilized, often by small imputations of inadequacy?

To understand masculine psychology archetypally, one must understand phallos and grasp how it is that the phallic archetype permeates male development and behavior.[1] Simply put, phallos is the governing symbol of masculinity. This present work is based upon foundational concepts detailed in my earlier work, *Phallos: Sacred Image of the Masculine*. Those concepts will not be discussed at length here, but in summary they are as follows:

1) Patriarchy is not the same as masculinity and must not be equated with it.[2] It is not necessary to diminish or to subordinate masculinity as one draws away from patriarchy. Quite the opposite.

2) Phallos is sacred to men as the manifestation of inner self. I use Mircea Eliade's notion of sexuality as "hierophany," as a means of understanding the holiness of phallos to men.

3) Phallos is co-equal with the feminine in origination. *Phallos protos*[3] is the psychological equivalent of the maternal uroboros[4] in

---

[1] Archetypes are primordial, structural patterns within the human psyche. According to Jung, "Archetypes are systems of readiness for action, and at the same time images and emotions. They are . . . . the chthonic portion of the psyche . . . that portion through which the psyche is attached to nature." ("Mind and Earth," *Civilization in Transition*, CW 10, par. 53) [CW in the footnotes refers to *The Collected Works of C.G. Jung*]

[2] By patriarchy I mean the evolutionary cultural stage of the past few thousand years, characterized by such themes as superiority of the masculine and the spiritual over the natural and the feminine, as well as dominance, submission, hierarchy.

[3] Archetypal masculine energy, co-equal with the archetypal feminine. See *Phallos: Sacred Image of the Masculine*, chapt. 4.

[4] Ancient image of a serpent biting its own tail, conveying the motif of the universal maternal womb, of as-yet undifferentiated beginnings of life.

the origin of life, and therefore also in the origin of psyche. Phallos is god in its masculine form.

4) Both solar (sun, light, spiritual) and chthonic (underworld, dark, material) phallos are sacred and essential to masculinity. All phallic—masculine—attributes are derived from the phenomenon of erection as enspirited flesh. This follows Jung's correlation of instinct and archetype. It is incorrect to value solar phallos and devalue chthonic phallos, since in Jung's understanding of the psychoid dimension of the archetype, polarities finally "transgress" one another, unifying the opposites.[5] To judge the one as superior and the other as inferior is, at the least, misleading.

5) The shadow of phallos, its negative and destructive element, is present in both solar and chthonic phallos.

To remove, damage or insult phallos is to remove, damage or insult a man's deepest sense of himself as a male person. This is castration, understood psychologically. Testes and phallos together comprise the masculine gender system and to my mind they are symbolically inseparable. Castration as I use the term means loss or injury to this system, denoted by its primary image, phallos. The Indo-European root of castrate is *kes*, to cut, to cut off from. *Kes* is the root also of chaste, empty, void.[6] To move from cutting to being cut off from, to chastity, to emptiness and the quality of voidness connects one with the psychological importance of castration for men. Castration as a metaphor refers to a man's deepest fear that his manhood might be lost or seriously compromised.

Until recently, only as individuals have men had to concern themselves with their vulnerability and status in living relationships. In social patterning, the patriarchal system has been intact and apparently dependable. The collective structures of patriarchy, expressing

---

[5] The term "psychoid" refers to the point of mystery and paradox where the material and the spiritual dimensions of life are One, where these opposites cross over into each other so that what is psychological is also physiological. See Jung, "On the Nature of the Psyche," *The Structure and Dynamics of the Psyche,* CW 8, par. 417.

[6] *American Heritage Dictionary,* p. 1523.

the rule of the masculine over the feminine and those males perceived to be weaker, have been pervasive in Western civilization. They have supported masculine gender identity. As women and oppressed men have become stronger, patriarchal assumptions of superiority have been seriously shaken.

In psychoanalytic thinking, reflecting Western culture generally, the feminine has been considered dominant in the unconscious, the masculine in consciousness. With the feminine emerging as a force in consciousness, a radical shift in contemporary awareness has taken place. Men are being pushed into an investigation of masculinity in the *un*conscious even as women are discovering feminine consciousness. A lodgement of masculinity in the unconscious requires an awareness of *phallos protos,* the basic and primal presence of the masculine in the psyche. Castration as loss, or intimation of loss, of phallos can then be seen as the catastrophic threat that it is for men.

Male rage, and the heralds of rage—discomfort, depression, dark moods, nastiness, anxiety and anger, to say nothing of hurt—are ubiquitous. Rage lurks beneath the surface of every man's composed behavior, ready to erupt when the appropriate button is pushed. No man is exempt, no matter how evolved his sensibilities, how contained his emotions, how educated his mind. Rage and its harbingers are not peculiar to men, to be sure, but there is a quality, a character, to male rage that is directly related to the ominous import of castration as a peculiarly male terror.

I believe that one can look at the behavior of males, and what masculine behavior symbolizes, from a specifically masculine point of view. I will use the phrase "masculine psychology" in these pages. Within the context of species, males and females are both human beings and share common characteristics of that species. My focus in this work is upon the most critical gender-specific issue for males. Quite obviously, therefore, I do not write about females. I consider the examination of masculine identity, behavior and meaning to be an authentic enterprise, without prejudice to the value and reality of its opposite.

Males and females are significantly different anatomically and biologically. It is my assumption that from these differences certain distinctions have evolved into the psychological characteristics of masculinity and femininity. The characteristics are gender-specific since their basis is biological: they are both instinctual and archetypal. Their presence within the psychologies of individual male and female persons, however, quite clearly crosses over the gender line.

Problems arise when either men or women examine life from their limited perspective and then attribute their findings to everyone—a major consequence of the power issue between the sexes. An additional danger is the equation of, say, masculine characteristics found in males with masculine characteristics found in females. Once these dangers are acknowledged and effectively guarded against, it is altogether legitimate to examine castration and male rage from within the context of masculine psychology.

In 1989 I was living in Zurich on a sabbatical leave from my practice, working on this book. One day I was in our kitchen making applesauce, essentially an easy and small job. My wife Barbara was peering over my shoulder giving me advice, telling me to pick the cloves from the apples before putting them into the food mill, etc., etc. I found myself saying—even though her advice made a simple task even easier—"Get your hands out of here." I consider myself something of an expert in applesauce, and she was interfering, improvement or no. I was quietly pleased at being able to say that to her in the kitchen, for those words were almost exactly what she has said to me any number of times when I putter around while she is seriously cooking. It was my chance to get even.

As soon as the words came from my mouth, however, something flashed. I had been reading Karen Horney, the early German-American Freudian analyst. In her essay "The Dread of Woman,"[7] Horney wrote that the origin of a man's fear of women is the mother's early forbidding of her infant son's fondling of himself, inhibiting his discovery of the pleasure that comes from penile stimulation. The boy, discovering his excitement at the play, is at the earliest

---

[7] *Feminine Psychology,* pp. 133-146.

stages of his own masculine self-discovery. His tiny exploratory efforts require a positive reaction or mirroring from his world—still effectively limited to the experience of his mother. Such mirroring sets the stage for a later coalescence within the boy of his nascent self, the basis for his masculine self-regard. Horney suggests that a boy moves on to feel sadistic impulses toward his mother and her body which are connected to the rage provoked quite spontaneously by her prohibition.

So there I am, standing in the kitchen, with all of this coursing through a mind apparently intent upon making applesauce. And I lay a gloss on Horney and say to myself that this whole thing is a good example of the truth of Freud's notion of infantile sexuality and its polymorphically perverse implications extended into incipient old age. I say to Barbara, in a kind of sarcastic jest, the words she has so often said to me—the self-same words that Freud and Horney claim are said, under one guise or another, to male babies who are discovering the presence and pleasure of their maleness.

A displacement has taken place; the applesauce is not a penis, nor is Barbara a son or I a mother. Yet the dynamics are there. With scant transposition, the words become, "Get your hands out of there," and they are a recrudescence of what may have been my infantile male wounding, a reminder of a forgotten message that I have no business being who I am—a phallically playful boy. I throw the words back at her as a defense according to the talion principle (an eye for an eye, a tooth for a tooth). My wound has been touched and a moment of regression has occurred.

The fact that I dashed to the typewriter to record this vignette for posterity is precisely what Freud calls sublimation, or the ability of the ego to deal with potentially explosive emergences of instinct by substituting a culturally acceptable means of gratification. Such a story makes one aware of how much the control of one's primary emotional response is dependent upon education and the development of consciousness, however fragile such accomplishments become in moments of intense threat—as mine, in this instance, was not.

I use the term "patriarchal design" to indicate a kind of strategic intelligence, not always conscious, which serves to obscure male vulnerability. Males are not to be vulnerable—to be surmountable, vincible, pregnable is to be feminine. Patriarchal design instigates the covert, unspoken contract males have with one another, taking for granted male superiority. The rudiments of male rage begin to form when male weakness can no longer be altogether hidden. Patriarchal design typically lays the responsibility for male rage at the feet of women, who supposedly prompt the rage by their closeness to the irrational and chthonic unconscious.

Is male rage actually masculine irrationality, or, better said, the terror a man feels at the psychological presence of the forbidden and terrifying feminine in the masculine unconscious? Or does male rage express a genuine masculine fear of losing one's most precious possession? Indisputably, rage comes from within a man, however women might contribute to igniting the flame. It is my contention that "the feminine" does indeed play a major part in male rage, but to think that this means confrontation with an outer feminine person, or even an inner feminine aspect of a male, is not the whole story. Withal, patriarchal design conspires to hide the rage, placing blame on women who supposedly provoke it. The major purpose is to defend against the implications of femininity in and for a man. Not surprisingly, expressions of rage do the opposite.

Femininity is a terror for men, since females have no apparent phallos. The implication of subjective femininity suggests castration. For men, the specter of being feminine is based on the perception that femininity emerges when the annihilation of masculinity takes place by means of castration.

In chapter one, this work will examine the psychological construction of the masculine grid within the psyche through a discussion of the transformations necessary for its formation.

Castration, the classic metaphorical impairment of masculine formation, will be discussed in chapter two, as seen through the images of Freud and Jung. Castration cannot be understood within its psychoanalytic context without a clear understanding of Freud. By the same token, the metaphorical importance of castration cannot be understood by modern persons without reference to Jung, who took Freud's physiological and concrete/historical conceptualizations and made of them a way of symbolic entrance into the unconscious.

Chapter three will take up six ways in which males experience castration: as imposed by other men, by women, by themselves, by fate, by society and, finally, ontologically.

Chapter four will discuss rage as a concomitant of castration. Castration anxiety and threat is a way of understanding the universality of male rage.

Chapter five will be a discussion of antidotes for castration and rage, a discussion that is but an opening of the door.[8]

Read on, men, and hold your groin if the spirit moves you. Women, read on, and understand your men as vulnerable and frightened and hell-bent on protecting themselves.

---

[8] Two important issues are beyond the scope of this work: circumcision and female animus injury. Male circumcision, especially as an adolescent rite of passage, is an heroic trial. Animus castration implications can perhaps be deduced from what are here seen as major junctures in the development of maleness, but they properly belong to a work on feminine psychology.

1
Masculinity and Transformation

As mentioned in the introduction, the material presented here depends for its foundational concepts upon my earlier work, *Phallos: Sacred Image of the Masculine*. The reader who knows that book is prepared to understand how it is that concrete or metaphorical damage to phallos has a catastrophic connotation for men. In that book, phallos is held to be the masculine god-image—the symbol, and thus, as in Jung's understanding of symbol, the actuality of what we call masculine identity.

Jung wrote that "the true symbol . . . should be understood as an expression of an intuitive idea that cannot yet be formulated in any other or better way."[9] Again:

> The raw material shaped by thesis and antithesis, and in the shaping of which the opposites are united, is the living symbol. Its profundity of meaning is inherent in the raw material itself, the very stuff of the psyche, transcending time and dissolution; and its configuration by the opposites ensures its sovereign power over all the psychic functions.[10]

Physical, concrete phallos is Jung's "raw material." As I understand phallos symbolically, the opposition Jung mentions can be seen not only as the difference between physical phallos and its metaphorical implications in the male psyche; it can also be seen as chthonic (sensual) versus solar (spiritual) masculine energy, often considered to be polar opposites. In either case, as base data from which symbol emerges, phallos is the starting point. Phallos conveys a "profundity of meaning," as one discerns in it the convergence of both body and symbol. "An intuitive idea" moves one beyond the

---

[9] "On the Relation of Analytical Psychology to Poetry," *The Spirit in Man, Art, and Literature*, CW 15, par. 105.
[10] "Definitions," *Psychological Types*, CW 6, par. 828.

stalemate of either/or, concrete or symbolic, profane or sacred. As such, phallos is not only the means of grasping the mystery of masculine identity, but, as Jung's "raw material," it is what it signifies.

The term "castration" is often used to denote the loss of the testes only, but in my use, as noted in the introduction, testes and penis are two elements in a single masculine reproductive and symbol system and cannot be separated. Taken metaphorically, castration means to emasculate, which, since there are but two genders, is subjectively computed by the male as feminization.

I assume that physical masculinity and psychological masculinity are interdependent qualities, and that it is quite impossible to speak of one without thereby implying the other. Loss of physical and/or symbolic masculinity is therefore the loss of what is essential for manhood. Phallos as energized penis—with testes implied—is the expression of transcendence understood from within a masculine frame of reference. Phallos is definition, expression and meaning, so basic to masculine identity and behavior that it is impossible to know or comprehend maleness apart from it. Jung wrote: "The phallus is the source of life and libido, the creator and worker of miracles, and as such it was worshipped everywhere."[11]

Every man has a personal connection with his own sexual organ, one of which he rarely speaks. His capacity to pass the fabric of life on to another generation is inextricably connected to his sexuality. His phallos expresses his creative power. It is his means of entering the body, the experienced reality, of another person. It is also the instrument of his passion and the provider of ecstasy, giving an experience, however anticipatory, of ontological transcendence. These three elements—creation, joining with another and ecstasy—are common ground binding together the opposites of sensuality and spirituality, making phallos the uniting symbol that it is.

Here is an example of how the concrete and the metaphorical coalesce. Patrikyia deWicce, in a lovely short article, tells of her failed marriage in Boston, after which, in her forties, she moved to Maine.

---

[11] *Symbols of Transformation,* CW 5, par. 146.

18 *Masculinity and Transformation*

There she met a woodsman some years her senior. A long and delicious love-affair began, ended by his death. The connection changed her life; she ripened "into full sexuality." She reveals the zinger. The man was essentially impotent. He had, in his lovemaking, used his "soft and gentle paw."[12]

Phallos, therefore, need not always require concrete phallos, however necessary phallos is as the basic image. If the inner phallic nature of the man is intact and hungry, his personality and his entire body become phallos. Celibate men who are constitutionally phallic are genuinely masculine.

Jung wrote that "a phallic symbol does not denote the sexual organ, but the libido, and however clearly it appears as such, it does not mean *itself* but is always a symbol of the libido."[13] In Jung's understanding of psychic energy, libido includes such elemental human requirements as creativity, connection with the "other," and ecstasy, the spiritual movement from ego to Self. Viewed from a masculine perspective, libido, identified as it is with phallos, finds no other subjective source of definition apart from the energized symbol of male gender.

A man lies in bed at night wondering about life, about who he is, about reality as contained within his personal experience. His hand finds his organ and he touches it, recalling his own encounters with transpersonal connection. The object of his touching is not simply his sexual organ per se. His touching is his means of establishing himself with himself, of reconnecting with memory, his "linking-back," the meaning of religion. It is, indeed, the means of soul, soul-bearing, soul-ownership.

Jung's movement beyond phallos as concrete human penis/erection toward its importance as a symbol of libido might be taken to indicate that matter and spirit are essentially separate entities, rather than two dimensions of the same psychic—and psychoid—reality. A male's realization of creativity, the start of a new generation, inti-

---

[12] "A Soft and Gentle Paw," pp. 5-6.
[13] *Symbols of Transformation,* CW 5, par. 329.

macy with an other (entry into another's body) and orgasmic ecstasy all have their roots in his sexuality. The relationship between concrete phallos and symbolic libido thus becomes clear.

Transgressivity, the crossing of boundaries, is a characteristic of the psychoid nature of the archetype and surely related to transformation. Jung, in *Symbols of Transformation*, the work that marked his separation from Freud, took pains to establish the transformational aspect inherent in symbolism. Symbols, in their deepest dimension, do not simply point to another reality. In a specific sense, they are a container for that reality; they express it, convey it. One initiated in and alive to the Christian eucharistic sacrament, for example, does not hold in hand a piece of bread that "stands for" the presence of Christ. Christ is in the bread; Christ is the bread; the bread is Christ. The inner, invisible form of the object is revealed by the ritual of consecration. Ordinary bread is symbol. Similarly, phallos—not only as sexual organ but as sexual organ expressing psychic energy, as expression of creativity, intimacy and ecstasy—is a libido symbol. And the manifestation of masculine identity and experience. Thus the concrete object (penis) is simultaneously symbol (phallos).

Phallos is profoundly known to be symbolic by men, whether or not they can explain their knowledge. The polarities of materiality-sexuality-instinct and spirituality-symbol-archetype and their reunion, so to speak, are expressed by Jung in alchemical language as the *coniunctio oppositorum*.[14] Coniunctio conveys the secret that is hidden behind appearance, in the soul. Whereas consciousness requires a separation of opposites, the union of opposites is a psychological reality under the surface, awaiting a moment of revelation and incarnation. Transformation is present in everything if one can see it.

Indeed, transformation is a fundamental law of the psyche. It is especially crucial to an understanding of masculinity, since the change that takes place in a man's body when penis becomes phallos

---

[14] An alchemical motif symbolizing psychic processes involving the union of opposites, joining in the unconscious and giving the potential of something new emerging into consciousness. Paradoxically, the *coniunctio* is a goal of the alchemical/psychological work, and yet beyond attainment.

is classically illustrative of change of form. The strange, even mysterious, even startling alteration in size and structure of the penis when it is charged with sexual energy indicates the presence of transpersonal force. The motif of transformation is typical to masculine development in general, taking as its cue the unpredictable and autonomous behavior of the masculine member. The relationship between phallos and divinity for men rests upon this transformational aspect—a parallel to the excitement a man has in his erotic flash, and the psychological importance of arousal. It is no wonder that phallos is sacred to men, and that masculinity cannot be understood apart from a male's experience of transformation.

The Masculine Grid

To lay a groundwork for understanding masculine transformation, a discussion of what I have come to call the masculine grid is necessary. The grid, the inner phallic configuration of masculinity, is formed through several stages of transformation which take place in a male's development. I imagine a structure of phallic identity forming, strand crossing strand, in and through a male's critical masculinity-building life episodes. A frame begins to take shape, its strength depending upon the effect of the individual experiences which confirm or deny a gender-syntonic grasp of Self. The grid is never impermeable, since spaces exist between the strands, spaces which are wider, narrower, longer, shorter, depending upon the personal history—and the archetypal inheritance—of the individual.[15]

As development occurs, the grid presumably becomes stronger and gradually more dependable, until, at some point, it is possible for the boy-man to understand himself to be confidently male and clearly within the psychological field of phallos. There may be weak links in the grid, inadequate joining of strands, indeed strands that

---

[15] Although the material here regarding the masculine grid focuses on environmental conditions rather than dispositional factors, I do not mean to imply that the latter are unimportant.

are altogether missing. In any grid there are large or small spaces, permitting intrusions into consciousness from below. There may also be lacunae or "holes" in the fabric of the grid itself, which correspond to missing elements essential to masculine formation. Flowing though the lacunae may be aspects of the feminine that escape the transformations that will be discussed further on.

The notion of "grid" as an image of inner masculine coalescence has a symbolic appropriateness. After the example of phallos, standing as it does in a (more or less) straight line at a right angle to a man's trunk, masculinity is a linear psychological quality, even as circularity, after the example of womb and breast, is feminine. Further, the squares formed by intersecting rods or strands suggest masculine wholeness even as the circle traditionally suggests the feminine. A grid also suggests firmness, certainly a phallic characteristic, a framework upon which one can depend, providing the interlocking parts are properly in place and well connected. Skyscrapers, the American urban phallic symbol par excellence, were not possible until a grid of structural steel could be formed upon which the walls and floors of such buildings might be supported. While one cannot precisely compare such constructions with an inner masculine phallic requirement, a certain correspondence exists.

The construction—in some cases, the reconstruction—of the masculine grid can be observed in the dreams of men for whom this issue is of paramount importance. One man, a Christian minister sexually drawn to males, whose work in therapy has been to possess his masculine inheritance, had this short but powerful dream message:

> Billy was in bed with me, putting his hand on my penis. He is looking at whatever is going on in the room. He is not coming on to me sexually. I am not sexually attracted. I am not aroused. His hand is holding me at the base of my penis.

Billy is the highly masculine, late teen-aged son of an old friend, handsome, virile, fresh, full of young male energy. Ordinarily, in conscious life, this kind of young man was precisely the masculine image to which my analysand was attracted—the object of his fantasy life. Billy's interest in the dreamer is not erotic, but it is related to the dreamer's masculinity, as evidenced by Billy's holding onto the dreamer's penis. Billy needs a connection with the parson's masculine grid, his inner substance. The dreamer, contrary to his predilection, is not erotically stimulated. Something is happening in this brief vignette that is altogether masculine, but not dominated by sexual desire.

The dream tells me that something of great importance is happening in the intrapsychic structure of my analysand. His masculine grid is coming together. He is not aroused by the closeness, the touching, the reaching-out of a beautiful young man. His own masculine structure is coalescing. He is becoming a man himself. The need for an erotic connection with a male to compensate for his weak masculine links is diminishing. He is not turned on by "the other," since "Billy" is no longer an "other." He and Billy are potentially the same.

Some ten years before his work began with me, an analysand dreamed that he saw two men with three-foot steel matrices in their hands. Someone said: "This is how we plow the earth now." Plowing the earth is an archetypal phallic activity. Our work on the dream suggested that the point of the image was to indicate the dreamer's newly emerging awareness of a more basic, rooted masculinity.

The establishment of a secure foundation of male identity is the aim of the masculine grid. After conceiving this notion, I found that Patricia Reis had written in 1986 that the feminine process of reaching the Great Goddess involves "peeling back layers, dissolving the 'grids' and exposing the deeper, underlying structures."[16] Reis's grids are patriarchal constructs that inhibit feminine self-realization. This conceptualization is somewhat different from mine, to be sure, but it is interesting to note that in reflecting on the masculine her imagination led her to a similar configuration. "The grid," states Deanne Newman, "is the androcentric view of the world, seeing

---

[16] "The Mysteries of Creativity: Self-Seeding, Death, and the Great Goddess."

things from the male point of view."[17] Men need to develop their masculine grid, to see things from a male point of view. Women need to move beyond its imposition upon them by patriarchy.

A note here: David Miller of Syracuse University has made an important distinction between archetype and stereotype.[18] He points out that both describe pattern. A stereotype is common knowledge, usually oversimplified, often tired and worn. An archetype is an original model, an ideal form, to which similar things or actions are compared. Stereotypes may or may not be accurate reflections of the archetypal original; often they carry the implication of inferiority. Stereotypic conditioning is so pervasive that one cannot help but fall into it in one's thinking and writing, even when one intends the opposite. My intention is that the following descriptions of masculine transformation be archetypal, not stereotypic.

Six Stages of Masculine Transformation

Masculine development requires transformation from the beginning to the end of a man's life. In six critical life-periods an adequate transformational process makes the difference between strong masculine evolution or weakness in the masculine grid. A man can be a man without complete accomplishment in any one period, but a substantial achievement must take place if there is not to be an impairment in gender identity and his sense of well-being.

Freud was correct, I believe, in emphasizing the anxiety a man feels when there is an incomplete establishment of masculinity. Without such an establishment, there is forever the implication of unachieved masculinity, therefore of femininity. Femininity is not a problem in females. But until the sixth and final stage of masculine development, it is universally considered to be an issue in a man's expression of masculinity.

---

[17] I am grateful to Deanne Newman, analyst-in-training, in whose thesis on female empowerment and phallic awareness I discovered Reis.
[18] "World Peace: The Influence of the Unconscious."

Prenatal

In the prenatal period, all embryos are female morphologically until the sixth week, when the genetic predisposition supplied by the male parent releases testosterone if the embryo is to be male, and gonadal destiny is determined. Labia tissue merges to become scrotum; the penis grows from what otherwise would remain clitoris. Male development in the embryo would appear to be an addition, a modification, a transformation of a process that otherwise would have naturally produced a female person. It appears that alteration is intrinsic to masculine development from the onset of fetal life, ontogenetically. Change is an indigenous masculine characteristic.

Interestingly, this original transformation does not correspond to Freud's assumption that the female body is the focus of change, that the female's is the body without the penis and testicles, and therefore lacking in that which is crucial to normalcy. To the contrary, from a biological perspective the female would seem to be normative—the male's apparatus an addition. Castration, then, cannot be considered, as did Freud, as something that "has been done" to the female; it represents the ever-present threat to masculinity of a reversal of the addition of maleness, a return, a regression, to primal femininity. Masculinity and "additionality" are correlative concepts, and it may well be that every important ingredient in masculine psychology stems, essentially, from this basic configuration. With regard to the transformation of penis into phallos—the heart of the matter—it puts one in mind of Jung's quotation from Goethe's *Faust* (with a nice concomitant of the numinosity phallos understandably has for a man), "It glows, it shines, increases in my hand!"[19]

Castration as "absence" is thus a factor in the earliest stage of male differentiation. Does this mean, I ask myself, that masculinity is a secondary and derivative phenomenon built upon a fundamental basis of "the feminine"? This is not clear from my earlier work on phallos, but I must admit that the prenatal body-priority of the feminine causes me to pause and to wonder. I suspect that in this ques-

---

[19] *Symbols of Transformation*, CW 5, par. 180.

tion I am caught in my own tendency to get stuck in linear thinking, whereas my intuition requires me to press toward a parity in gender origination. There can be no "being" (feminine) without "doing" (masculine), even as there can be no "doing" without "being."

Pre-oedipal

A second transformational period occurs when a boy baby, in what Freud calls his "sexual researches," discovers pleasurable sensations in the manipulation of his penis. This transformation turns on a boy's dawning awareness that he has a penis, that the penis is enjoyable, and that a subjective enjoyment of penis has to do with being a boy. A boy's discovery that he is a boy parallels his discovery that his mother is not a boy. A girl child also discovers, at some point, that she is different from her mother, but the difference is one of personhood, not of gender.

Male gender differentiation is my focus in this stage of development, the knowledge that comes to a boy that he belongs to a breed apart from his mother. Freud put great stock in this discovery, since the boy's dawning awareness that females have no penis, together with the implications of punishment stemming from the prohibition of masturbation, are for Freud the basis of male castration anxiety. Thus, the emergence of castration anxiety coincides with and at the same time contradicts a boy's fledgling awareness of his maleness.

Geneticists John Money and Anke Ehrhardt write that "gender-dimorphic [two-body] signals and expectancies"[20] are transmitted to a child during the pre-oedipal period. Developmentally, they call the tipping of the scales in a boy toward maleness "virilization," reflecting Freud's picture of the boy discovering the pleasure of masturbation. Virilization functions in cooperation with prenatal genetic programming to carry over into post-birth growth the establishment of the masculinization of gender. The point is that both genetic formation and early conditioning conspire to differentiate gender identity in the male child, serving as the beginning of a process of confirming a

---

[20] *Man and Woman, Boy and Girl*, p. 16.

boy's "private experience of gender."[21] Money and Ehrhardt write: "The noteworthy years are from the onset of language acquisition, at around eighteen months, until between age three and four."[22] This change from a neuter identity, synonymous with Freud's original bisexuality, into one of beginning identity as a male is critical.

Pre-oedipal transformation denotes a boy's beginning sense of difference from his source, his self-object in Kohut's terms, his mother—from whom he has received not only the gift of life but upon whom he has depended for a reflection of himself as a nascent person. Seen in that light, it is perhaps better said that a boy's earliest experience of gender is really not neuter but female, a mirroring of the gender of his mother. It is against this earliest and primal identification that masculine gender establishment must contend. I consider this second step in the masculine transformational process to be a recapitulation, in experience, of the original masculine "change" in utero.

To understand the urgency of this second step, it is necessary to bear in mind the importance of the mother, or mother surrogate, as the initial conveyor of separate personhood to each child to whom she gives birth, or primarily cares for. Erich Neumann characterized this primary caring need:

> The child's initial powerlessness and total dependence on the mother in the primal relationship gives her an "archetypal" position. No matter how the infant experiences her physically, she is the surrounding world in which and from which it lives.[23]

Neumann calls this phase "matriarchal," one in which "every single 'too much' or 'too little' beyond the appropriate range is experienced as negative by the child."[24] It is at this point that personal value begins as an inner, psychological reality for the child. This is the initial gestalt of the self—or non-self, when negative mirroring

---

[21] Ibid., p. 4
[22] Ibid., p. 16.
[23] "Fear of the Feminine," p. 7.
[24] Ibid., p. 8

predominates—upon which all subsequent experiences are built. Thus, through the interpersonal connection with the mother, the first knowledge of individual existence and suggestions of gender identity coincide.

Here is an explanation for the critically important correspondence of masculine identity and basic self-regard in a male's later years. The two occur simultaneously and are thereafter inextricably interrelated, and very likely interdependent, as foundation elements in a male's individual impression of himself and his personal validity. A male's pre-oedipal discovery of phallos remains in his psychological system throughout his years as a propensity to masturbate, seen as a primary-process establishment of his early discovery and personal affirmation of difference. A mother can help to establish her son's gender-otherness by her love and acceptance of her boy-child, with his proclivity to play with himself. She can provide a base for his beginning masculine grid, his inner sense of identity as a male.

The father, at this point, would seem to be secondary in importance to the mother, essentially aiding and supporting a process that finds its center in her. His relationship to the mother, however, is critical in that his support influences her sense of femininity, her mothering, her satisfaction at having produced a male child who is so different from herself. If the father's relationship with the mother is antithetical, producing a negative attitude in the mother toward him, something of this negativity will be communicated to the son. It is a serious error for a father to believe that his negligence toward his wife has no repercussion on their son. Fathers represent masculinity to their wives and their children, whether overtly or covertly. In the case of infant boys the value of the presence in the mother's life of a strong, attendant and dependable masculine presence is incalculable.

No one knows at what point a boy-child begins to absorb masculine essence directly from the father—an opposite to the mother's all-encompassing, defining omnipresence, resonating with the young impulses burgeoning from his son. The beginnings of consciousness at the son's early age involve an awareness of gender difference. The son becomes subject, the mother becomes object; from this distinction comes sexual desire, the primal impulse toward the hunger for an opposite, the instinctual—and archetypal—wellspring of individuation as described by Jung. Fathering is sensed by the boy as something different from mothering, a truly important click in perception, introducing a distinction into awareness at a very early point. Money and Ehrhardt may have had something of this sort in mind when they wrote of "gender-dimorphic signals and expectancies" transmitted to the child in the first years of life.

Oedipal

In the oedipal period, between the third and sixth years, a most critical transformational dynamic in early masculine development takes place. More males are lost at this stage of transformation than at any other. Since this important alteration in masculine development is central to an understanding of Freud's castration theory, it will be discussed extensively in chapter two rather than at this point. Here it is sufficient to state a brief outline of the change that occurs.

The boy-child, until his oedipal crisis and its resolution, continues to be psychologically attached to his mother. Freud claims that the boy is in love with his mother, drawn to her, desirous of her, powered by his instinctual nature. (One must remember at this point that the boy is still psychologically bisexual; he is torn between his phallic enjoyment and his identification with his mother-producer.) The boy is already aware of his penis and of the ability it has to give him pleasure. He is also becoming aware of his father's connection to his mother, as her opposite and erotic partner, and the boy's opponent.

The issue at this juncture is the boy's dissociation from the mother as a projection of the boy's own self-image, a radical disjuncture in his personal identification process. The boy must further understand himself as a creature different from his mother, an advance in the inner coalescing of his masculine grid. The mother is eased, or perhaps, as she feels it, brutalized, out. The boy finds himself alone and bereft, but a boy. The mother may have invited the symbiosis, a quite natural impulse, but it is the father's responsibility to put a stop to it. Failure on the part of one parent spells difficulty; failure on the part of both is a sign of impending disaster.

On the other hand, if all goes relatively well the boy moves into what Freud calls the latency period, and the whole matter of sexual desire goes underground, working itself out in subliminal ways. The boy plays out his sprouting masculinity in games with his buddies, in avoiding girls, and in being disobedient to his mother. The father's role as castrating enforcer of the incest taboo, as well as the importance of his reconstitutive relationship with his son, will be dealt with further on.

Adolescent

This period begins in puberty and extends through a male's subsequent thirty-odd-year management of the consequences of physical and sexual maturation. A man is psychosexually an adolescent until his libido moves beyond the simple concreteness of its pubertal focus into accomplishment and individuation.

An adolescent young man moves out and away from his family, but he may also move dangerously more closely in. Classically, he moves out, a recrudescence of oedipal energy, but with a surrogate mother figure, the girl friend, unencumbered by the incest taboo. Early interests of the boy-child reemerge. "The driving force," wrote Freud, "which this male portion of his body will generate later at puberty expresses itself in childhood essentially as an impulsion to inquire into things—as sexual curiosity."[25]

Curiosity is flagrant in puberty. If it is not, notice should be taken by parents. If a boy's curiosity is frustrated, his maleness can be stunted, fearful, intimidated. Since Jung, of course, introversion no longer has a bad name, a suggestion of impending illness about it. It is an authentic typological attitude, and can be one's natural bent. All the same, young men are typically energized by outer challenge. The fascination of the feminine, a need to prove, an awakened desire to create, are libido symbols of an ignited phallos. The boy-now-young-man produces hundreds of thousands of seed in his testes

---

[25] Quoted by Karen Horney in *Feminine Psychology,* p. 139.

daily, and the transformation thus engendered has monumental ramifications. Harold Kelman quotes Karen Horney:

> Now one of the exigencies of the biological differences between the sexes is this—that the man is actually obliged [I would say by the fate of his gender physiology] to go on proving his manhood to the woman. ... The man ... has to *do* something in order to fulfill himself. The ideal of "efficiency" is a typical masculine ideal ... oriented toward the materialistic, the mechanistic, toward action.[26]

This revolution begins at puberty. It is altogether different for the female, whose ovulation begins at about the same time but is limited to twelve cycles a year, one egg a cycle, for, say, forty years—a total of some 480 ova. Moreover, the female need "do" nothing with her egg. The male must "do" something with his sperm. Unless the male can manage erection and delivery, necessarily an action requiring phallos, there is no adventure in creativity, intimacy, ecstasy. The psychological implications of this biological distinction are enormous.

The playfulness of latency becomes the sexual play of the teenager and then the adult man. The difference is that phallic thrust is frank and obvious. The onset of puberty sets a male on a course for thirty years. He seeks sexual partners who provide him with self-knowledge and self-expression.

Accomplishment

Between late adolescence and, say, age 35, a process takes place in a man's life that is surely transformative, but in a non-erotic, non-instinctual direction. This might be called the "work" transformation as opposed to the "love" transformation of adolescence. One must be careful here. This necessary transition in masculine psychology can be mistakenly understood as the whole rather than a part. Neumann, for example, has done this in his insistence upon solar masculine qualities as the goal of masculine development. Jungians, generally, tend to take this attitude. It is, however, important in this stage that

---

[26] "Introduction to Horney," ibid., p. 30. See also below, pp. 48-49.

accomplishment become a way in which genital phallic energy is also expressed, that a man's sexuality broadens out to include any number of metaphorical menifestations.

In this transformation, the energy nature pours forth in concrete sexual capacity and appetite is substantially converted into allegorical phallic activity. This is Freud's concept of sublimation. Choosing a vocation, finding a wife and establishing a family, accumulating property, taking leadership in organizational life are all traditional, metonymic equivalences of phallos. Erotic desire is by no means gone, but much of it (too much, in many instances) is rechanneled.

If the transformation is seriously flawed, a man remains slavishly chained to pubescent erotic drive, unable to establish himself within an adult world. Unable, even, to find an occupation. The primal call of instinct remains undeveloped and unfocused in work. The man drifts, moving from pleasure to pleasure, or pleasure-substitute to pleasure-substitute, with his adolescent hand outstretched. Masculine pride in accomplishment never seriously takes place.

A man requires a sense of attainment as coefficient to his phallic nature since attainment for a man is parallel to erection and insemination. He must, in Horney's words, prove himself. Without the proof, there is an implication of impotency-femininization-castration. The fifth transformation is thwarted.

The "too much" two paragraphs above has to do with the enticements offered men in Western society to trade the satisfactions of creativity, entrance into "the other" and ecstasy—three promises of phallos—for social standing and collective approval. Impairment of the body and imprisonment in ego satisfaction are the product—the selling of one's soul to the demon of worldly status. When religion is effective, its transcendent values at least provide some resistance against ego seduction.

A man's need to prove himself is integral to masculine psychology. The roster of desired accomplishments varies, but once a man has entered into this transformation, he requires a sense that he amounts to something in his community, that he is recognized by competitive peers, that he "phallically belongs."

Individuation

By the age of forty, say, pubertal transformation is usually established, with a serious leg up on accomplishment. An adult counterpart of infantile phallic narcissism has taken place—pride in oneself, in one's masculine stature, in the appreciation of one's own image, all producing masculine self-regard.

Ordinarily men take this process for granted, so deeply imbedded is it in the development of the masculine grid. Men spend their time comparing notes with each other on how far they have gone, how far someone else has gone, how disastrously so-and-so has slipped in the climb toward masculine attainment. They read the papers with an eye on comparison. This measurement of variables has as its source the movement out of latency into sexual adequacy, the cosmic change that comes upon a boy who enters young manhood with a budding phallos upon which he can depend and with which he can offer himself to the world with a measure of inner confidence. Early manhood circumambulates around the vicissitudes of physical and psychological erection, put into place to accomplish a task, both actual and metaphorical.

At the sixth stage, we meet the mid-life crisis in a man. I will deal with two aspects of this crisis: one might be called remedial, where a man must "go back" and attend to unfinished aspects of prior stages of development; the other is individuational, a movement onward toward life's completion. The two have much to do with one anther; almost always remedy and individuation coincide. Both involve transformation; on the one hand the repair of one's masculine grid, and on the other the grid itself becoming the loom for a new fabric.

Repair in the mid-life crisis attends to when and where a man passed the time of a prior phallic transformation without having accomplished its important tasks. Undone work hangs over his shoulder, haunting him. For example, if the childhood oedipal disconnection from the mother has left hangovers of childish dependence, large psychological "chunks" of identification with her remain. It may seem preposterous to a grown man that his problem may be a legacy from his mother-boundness, but this is what Jung means when he refers to an infantile attitude in adult men. The exaggerated and debilitating need to be protected, cared for, constantly nourished—projected upon wife, corporation, children who are struggling to establish themselves—becomes destructive, even pathological, self-pity.

As one rushes through the earlier transformations, an imperious, demanding toddler slips through the cracks, often emerging later when a complex has been touched. When the mid-life crisis attacks, the baby part of the man is unmasked as a factor in the adult personality, often with striking clarity. Stock market victories, property acquisition, professional attainment, gifted children, are revealed as substitutes for maternal nurturance. When the curtain of false self-reliance—what might be called pseudo-phallos—is parted, weakness in the masculine grid is exposed as a devastating, deep-seated despair, castration as impotence.

A man's age at the onset of mid-life, entry into the so-called second half of life, is, of course, approximate. It may be thirty-five; it may be fifty. But that a crisis will occur in the man who failed to negotiate a prior stage of transformation is a surety. A man can cover his own sense of self-doubt, his fear of inconsequentiality, his lurking sense of masculine incompleteness for only so long. Disguises, compensations, substitutions may hide his lack of inner phallic strength, but there can be no long-term avoidance of psychological impotence. The structure of the grid wobbles.

A man at the mid-point of life might go into analysis because he feels great pain, sorrow, stuckness. He is angry, restless, defeated, faint. Analysis deals with his pain, helps him come to grips with feeling and emotion, ferrets out his "reasons." This first phase of analysis is generally reductive and deals with the past. A man must discover where he has been cheated, and where he himself has cheated, in his transformations.[27] He must, in a way, go through the transformations again, clearing the woods.

---

[27] See Daryl Sharp, *The Survival Papers: Anatomy of a Midlife Crisis,* for a dramatic account of this process.

Jung's second phase of analysis is not so much analytical and remedial as it is prospective and synthetic. Jungian work may never be totally prospective. There is a stubborn tendency within us to keep things as they are, to avoid the sacrifices necessary to embrace rebirth. But when and if synthesis occurs, the emphasis is upon individuation. So important was individuation to Jung that he called it an instinct, as deeply embedded in the psyche as the two biological instincts, self-preservation and the perpetuation of the species.

The peculiar transformation of individuation begins when one is ready, when enough of the prior work has been done, when something "slides over" in the unconscious, when what we have accomplished is not enough. Pain is not absent. Pain and movement are always coincident; suffering is a catalyst for development. In Jungian work, as in life, male individuation builds upon a successful establishment of masculinity. Individuation is not the repair of an earlier failure. It is an altogether different configuration, a reversal of the previous changes both in image and in energic direction. This final transformation requires a turning into, rather than away from, precisely what has heretofore been avoided: the subjective feminine, the antithesis of phallic manifestation and prowess.

Individuation is the urge in all human beings to differentiate themselves from collective or traditional patterns of self-understanding, and to make a journey peculiarly theirs, deeply personal, essentially mythic. Individuation can begin long before mid-life. It can begin at any point in life, or at no "point" at all. As with the biological instincts, its foundation is present from the beginning. However, at mid-life, pressure builds in a man to accomplish a task which seems to be contradictory to his earlier efforts at phallic attainment. Wholeness is the issue here, a new and strangely unsettling definition of masculinity. Wholeness is a step beyond bald phallic presence. Wholeness includes a man's subjective inclusion of the feminine, the contrasexual opposite, not in another person but in himself. Jung calls this opposite in a male the anima.

My focus on masculine individuation in this sixth transformational stage is the integration of a man's own feminine being within his extant phallic masculine grid. The presence in a male of strong feminine characteristics is a problem in previous transformational stages. There, subjective femininity inhibits phallos. But in the stage of individuation, what was heretofore a danger becomes a psychological necessity, even a blessing. It cannot be overemphasized that the integration of the inner feminine in the second half of life requires an already extant and functioning masculine grid. Phallic inner presence is the precondition for integrating the feminine.

This basic requirement of individuation may at first seem hostile to a man's ego and counterproductive to the establishment of his masculinity—as indeed it would have been at earlier stages. For him now to find it incumbent upon himself to integrate the very characteristic he has labored against may itself feel castrating, a separation from, an abandonment of, phallos. Certainly it is an abandonment of patriarchy. It is not, however, an abandonment of phallos.

A man with a working masculine grid does not need patriarchy as his outer scaffolding; he has an inner structure. He may, for a time, feel confused and windblown, vaguely disloyal to the fraternity, odd. He is in the process of peeling himself away from outer collective supports. The challenge of individuation for such a man is exciting, once it is grasped, as have been the more obvious and prior challenges of his more youthful erections. The point is that a man can move beyond his sure position for the sake of his wholeness.

Individuation for a man has to do with his willingness to embrace in himself what, from a patriarchal perspective, seems like weakness and castration. To the patriarchal mentality, it *is* castration. To an evolved phallic mentality, it is not. It is recognition that phallos, while indisputably the male god, is not the only god of the universe. The second half of life is a resting time for male strength, an opportunity to acknowledge that phallos does not run everything. Individuation for a man is when he begins to know that phallos is only half of the fabric of life, and that he has the image of the other half within. It behooves a man to get to know that other half in preparation for a winding down, a softer time, a return to the mother.

A man's acknowledgment of his inner feminine nature need not be experienced as defeat. Properly understood, the emergence of the feminine in a man at this stage is a comfortable relaxation of hard-pressed effort. Phallos loves the feminine, searches for her, wants her. The *hieros gamos*, the sacred union about which Jung wrote in his alchemical studies, is the mystical joining of the opposites within the personality of an individual, a deeply introverted condition of wholeness. It may be understood through the image of an external marriage of the opposites, king and queen, phallos and vagina, male and female. Psychologically, however, the *hieros gamos* is an inner experience of completion, the reverse of the outer goal toward which phallos unrelentingly pressed in earlier years.

Jung's vision of what the inner marriage means for a man necessarily involves an intact masculine-phallic grid engaging a feminine personality, the anima, in oneself. The outer experience of erection and woman meeting in erotic embrace have an inner correlation, based upon the known and accomplished prototypes in a man's external adventures. In Jung's view, nature expresses and anticipates individuation. Chthonic phallos, underground, dark, passionate, dangerous, desirous, full of appetite and drive and demanding attention, is anticipatory to a male's growing understanding of himself as interior. He comes to discover his personal potential in combining his exterior phallic sexuality with his interior receptive capacity.

A moving description of the *hieros gamos* as the end of masculine transformation is found in Isak Dinesen's *Out of Africa*. The Kikuyu chief Kinanjui, a wizened old man who had been Dinesen's friend and who stood in her eyes for the dignity of the African people, lies on his deathbed in Kenya:

> Kinanjui's head and trunk were so emaciated that all the structure of his big skeleton stood forth, he looked like a huge dark wooden figure roughly cut with a knife. His teeth and his tongue showed between his lips. His eyes were half dimmed, milky in his dark face. But he could still see, and when I came up to the bed he turned his eyes on me and kept them on my face all the time that I was in the hut. Very very slowly he dragged his right hand across his body to touch my hand. He was in terrible pain, but he was still himself and was still carrying great weight, naked upon his bed. From the look

of him, I thought that he had come back from his journey triumphant, and had got all his cattle back with him, in spite of his Masai sons-in-law. I remembered, while I sat and looked at him, that he had had one weakness: he had been afraid of thunder, and when a thunderstorm broke, while he was in my house, he adopted a rodent manner and looked round for a burrow. But here now he feared no more the lightning flash, nor the all-dreaded thunder-stone: he had plainly, I thought, done his worldly task, gone home, and taken his wages in every sense. If he were clear enough in his mind to look back at his life, he would find very few instances in which he had not got the better of it. A great vitality and power of enjoyment, a manifold activity were at their end here, where Kinanjui lay still. "Quiet consummation have, Kinanjui,"—I thought.[28]

Kinanjui surrenders himself to the softness of death, binding up phallos in a pack, remembering through Dinesen's memory that he had not backed down on life. Throwing the pack over his shoulder, he moves on. At the end, he had gotten the cattle that were properly his, and then he lay down to die, never surrendering the weight of justice and ownership—his hardness. He moves his hand across his ravaged body to touch hers, allowing his eyes to meet hers in admiration and gratitude—his softness. It is a consummate expression of the dignity of a peaceful return to the source as mother, mission accomplished, in a male who peacefully enters that realm as an individuated man.

A closing caveat. One can write about six stages of masculine transformation as a natural process and give the impression that a linear design of certain invariable segments is a master-plan of masculine development. In a way, I am suggesting such a plan, in aid of providing a very broad outline of how something that each of us generally understands as masculinity comes to be differentiated from what we know, generally, as femininity. That we know the difference between the two is, to my mind, not simply a product of cultural programming, however much this has interfered with gender identity and value. Given this, the need is to give men a structural

---

[28] Pp. 336-337.

basis for their self-understanding, a word/image that corresponds intellectually with their deeply sensed interior masculine grid. For women, my scheme might provide a means of grasping phenomena they cannot know directly from their own experience.

But in another sense, the conceptualization of a "master-plan" can be misleading. The stages of masculine transformation "cross over" themselves in individuals; one (or more) might well lie atop or beneath another through years of a man's life. To understand such a scheme as "truth" is to reify it, to objectify a process that is intensely personal, a process with many atypical variations which are themselves based upon patterns that are either out of sight or out of favor.

All variations contain psychological truth. Conformation to an invented system does not by itself constitute truth or goodness, no matter how useful the system. Nor does nonconformity, in and of itself, constitute an error. This does not invalidate systems in aid of understanding, per se. It does mean that one must be quite careful that a system does not work against the very individuation process it is meant to serve. It is an old trick of patriarchal design to manufacture systems of interpretation, to insist upon their truth, and then to enforce conformity to them. That such dogmatic assertiveness is increasingly seen to be self-serving and antithetical to personal authenticity is a factor in the demise of patriarchy.

One must use imagination in order to find meaning, so long as imagination corresponds to reality, whether rational or nonrational. An imaginal device, such as "six stages of masculine transformation," stands or falls on the extent to which it supplies a plausibly rational guide to what is essentially a nonrational and mysterious process. My concept of "six stages" is clearly a phallic, linear, rational device. If mystery is damaged by its use, psyche is damaged, and the scheme becomes another example of the foolishness of artifice. In psychology, it is necessary to use imagination, since psyche becomes known to us by images that carry power, whether rational or otherwise (wise-in-another-way).

2
Castration in Freud, Jung and Others

The notion of castration in psychoanalytic theory came from Freud. Jung did not do more than occasionally mention it. By 1912, when Jung was writing *Symbols of Transformation,* the work that would separate the two men, Freud had established the idea of castration as essential to his theory of childhood sexuality.[29]

Freud has been harshly criticized in recent years, both in the media and in scholarly works, tending to create the impression that his groundbreaking views are passé, even foolish. Freud was flawed, as everyone is, by conditions of time, place and gender perspective. Still, he was a beautiful writer, a man of immense creative imagination. I am indebted to him for his work with the biological roots of masculine psychology, the importance he places upon body and body's instinct, and how this shapes behavioral patterns in men.

In preparation for this work, I tried to read Freud in a fresh, even naive way, putting aside my Jungian prejudices. Still, I write on Freud and two of his followers not as a Freudian, steeped in the literature, doctrines and arguments of classical psychoanalysis, but as a Jungian. I knew I could not understand masculine transformational development without inclusion of the castration issue, and certainly one cannot understand castration without Freud, however limiting one may find his concretistic and dogmatic biological approach.

Sigmund Freud

Freud's great contribution to the understanding of the psyche was to uncover the existence of infantile and childhood sexuality. His theory

---

[29] See "On the Sexual Theories of Children" (1908) and "Analysis of a Phobia in a Five-Year-Old Boy" (1909), *The Standard Edition of the Complete Psychological Works of Sigmund Freud* [referred to hereafter as *Complete Works*], vols. 9 and 10 respectively.

of instinct, which he called the most important part of psychoanalytic theory, was based upon his convictions about early development. For Freud, infancy encompasses the oral (age 0 to 2) and anal (1-1/2 to 3) stages. These two stages are characterized in contemporary psychoanalytic thinking as the pre-oedipal period. Childhood encompasses the phallic stage (3 to 6) and latency the later childhood period (6 to 12). The oedipal conflict occurs during the phallic stage, near the threshold of latency. The genital stage begins at puberty and continues throughout life.

Libido and phallos

Freud believed the penis to be the primary erotic organ for both sexes from the beginning of life. A boy's hands are drawn to his penis, at first by the excitement induced by being bathed; a girl discovers a similar pleasure from her penis-like clitoris. Freud thought that this "penis" is constitutionally the same in young males and females. It is the centrality of the penis, for Freud, that establishes castration in males as a basic threat and penis-envy in females as characteristic of their gender. The earliest manifestations of autoerotic stimulation in both sexes has to do with the sensitivity of the penis, whether this is taken to be the thing-in-itself in males or its abbreviated form in females. All of Freud's subsequent sexual theorizing revolves around this cardinal assumption.

Freud called the innate instinctual energy that flows into infantile sexual expression *libido,* a Latin word meaning pleasure, desire, lust. In Freud's later thinking, the sexual implications of libido became extended into a wider range of affirmative aspirations, which he called the life, or eros, instinct. Thanatos, the death or aggressive instinct, opposes it. For Freud, the core of libido was sexual desire, whether manifested positively or negatively, actively (masculine) or passively (feminine), at whatever stage of life. Freud considered penis—phallos in its energized form—as the focal point for the expression of libido. Words that Freud used to characterize the flow of libido from its ground to its accomplishment have phallic directedness underlying their meaning—libido has an *aim,* it strives for *gratifica-*

tion of biological need.

Here a caveat must be made. I understand Freud's grasp of the importance of phallos as being particularly valuable—even necessary—in an examination of masculine psychology. However, as one reads Freud one can see over and again that he worked from a masculine viewpoint and then extrapolated his conclusions into humankind in general, sometimes in the most fanciful ways.

Certain early childhood experiences of boys—such as the supposed shock of discovering that females have no penis, but a "wound" where the penis was assumed to have been—are applied in opposite ways to females. The centrality of the penis was so essential for Freud that he assumed girls are also shocked at this "discovery" and therefore castration also plays a major role in their subjective psychosexual development. According to Freud, castration is important to females not as a threat but as something that has already psychologically happened, a core notion in the concept of penis-envy. Girls are seen as expecting that their penile clitoris will grow into a full penis, and since it does not, the feminine attitude is essentially masochistic and inferior. Nowhere is Freud's personal and cultural bias so strongly evident as in the application of his castration reflections to feminine psychology.

Of course, Jung also extrapolated from his male experience, assuming female experience to be oppositional. We Jungians have seen in our own school that understanding the feminine as a reversal of the masculine does not lead to the reality of the feminine. Having so said, I find Freud's androcentric focus upon the penis to be helpful, even essential, to an understanding of masculine psychology.

The oedipal conflict

For Freud, the precursor of castration anxiety for a boy begins in the pre-oedipal oral and anal psychosexual stages. The male child discovers his penis through play and coincidentally finds himself propelled to become his mother's lover. Wishing to possess her physically in such ways as he has divined from his observations and intuitions about sexual life, he attempts to seduce her by showing her the male organ he is proud to possess.[30] The boy's experience of parental disapproval and the prohibition of enjoying what he has discovered—the naughtiness of masturbation—plus his discovery that females have no penis, introduces him to the gestalt of castration.

The oedipal drama is a primary turning point for boys, and the fear of castration is the turning point of the oedipal conflict. Only if one begins with Freud's foundational premise of the unconscious reality of infantile and childhood sexuality can one follow his argument in explaining male anxiety—which circulates constantly around the critical importance of castration threat in the oedipal drama.

In the Greek myth, Oedipus' father, Laius, was warned by an oracle that his son would one day kill him. Laius sent his infant child out to die, but he was found and adopted by Polybus, king of Corinth. When Oedipus was grown, he learned of his fate from another oracle, who added that he would also marry his mother. To avoid this ignominy, Oedipus fled Corinth, never again to see Polybus or his wife, whom he assumed were his actual parents. On his way, he met an unknown man with whom he quarrelled; Oedipus struck him with his staff and killed him. The man killed was Laius, Oedipus' natural father. Arriving in Thebes, Laius' home, Oedipus was able to answer the riddle of the Sphynx. As a reward for the city's deliverance from the monster, Creon (the king) gave Jocasta, Laius' widow and Oedipus' natural mother, to Oedipus to wife. In time, children were born, and Oedipus became a pillar of society.

A plague hit the city. The Oracle of Delphi declared that it could not cease until the murderer of Laius was driven from the city. Oedipus' inquiries led to his discovery that he was, himself, the murderer of his father and that Jocasta, his wife, was also indeed his mother. Jocasta hanged herself and Oedipus put out his own eyes. Blind, he went into exile and disappeared from the earth.

This story gives name to the best-known human predicament unearthed by Freud. Phallos is never mentioned in the myth, but phal-

---

[30] Freud, "An Outline of Psycho-Analysis," *Complete Works,* vol. 23, pp. 144-207.

los as instinct and as male sexual energy is everywhere active or hovering about in the drama. Freud believed that Oedipus' self-blinding was his metaphorical castration, a self-punishment for stumbling into incest and father-murder in spite of his consciously held good intentions. This is the stuff of genuine tragedy.

The story is universal because of its inevitability. A male cannot avoid the magnetic pull of his erotic connection with his mother—fate conspires to place him in a situation where his original dependence and love flow toward her. Freud believed her breast was a male's first erotic encounter. Additionally, a boy quite naturally feels antipathy to his father as a rival; and a father, if he is sensually connected with his wife, becomes jealous. He will not stand for his son's interference. The father's punishment for his son's interest in the mother/wife, or the implied threat of punishment, is the major source of castration anxiety.

The oedipal drama for a boy goes like this. Having more or less successfully passed through the pre-oedipal stages, he finds himself 1) aware of and pleased by his penis, and 2) in need of love from his mother, which together constellate a surge of erotic interest in her. His sexuality has emerged, not in conscious awareness, but in his over-all psycho-physiological constitution. Sexuality at the oedipal stage is veiled, but libido continues to rise in the boy's maturing process, and it impels him. Freud termed the mother a boy's love object, the result of her caring, empathetic mirroring of his separate reality in the pre-oedipal stages. The boy's gradual discovery of himself, a course which leads to a clearer primacy of penis in the oedipal stage, is responded to with an integrating and essentially positive affirmation by his parents (though the pre-oedipal masturbation prohibition works against this).

The boy thus becomes a competitor with his father for his mother's interest and admiration, for her desire. He wants to be the love preference of his mother, his mother's boy, first in her attention and affection. The fate of the division of sexual energy into two gendered bodies—phallic and penetrating for the boy, feminine and attracting for the mother—confirms the boy's growing sense of himself as a masculine person. His mother exerts a magnetic drawing power over him, carrying the process forward.

The oedipal drama is an inevitable and ubiquitous coming-together of libidinous elements scattered about in a male's previous stages of development. It is the core dynamism in Freud's understanding of a boy's psychosexual relationship both to his mother and to females generally. Everything leads up to it, and subsequently everything leads away from it, bearing critical traces of its resolution or irresolution. What happens in the oedipal conflict is critical in determining and qualifying a boy's sexual identity as well as establishing the foundation of his later psychological development.

Freud understood the oracular predictions in the myth as implicit castration metaphors. Laius attempted to avoid being murdered by his son; Oedipus attempted to avoid his fate as father-murderer and mother-seducer. Neither succeeded. Generally, a father feels the threat of death as exclusion if the son remains central within his mother's field of love. The son is caught in a terrible mother embrace, bonded to her, contained by her, for, failing the presence of a virile husband, she needs the son as much as the son wants her. If the son's libidinal tie to his mother is not broken, he is faced with the death of his masculinity, a reflection of his father's inability to intrude in the mother-son romance.

Death of the father and incest with the mother both compute, subjectively and unconsciously to the boy, as castration, the cutting off of life. Death of the father means that the son has no image of masculinity upon which he can model himself. Incest with the mother means that the son finds himself "inside" her. Physical incest, dominated by instinct, becomes the prototype of psychological incest, dominated by archetype. The result of psychological incest is the son's using the mother as model rather than the father, seeing the world through her eyes, sensing the world through her senses. Since she is feminine, such an identification is injurious to his discovery of himself as masculine.

Freud went further. Laius' sending away of Oedipus, abandoning him, to avoid disaster, is itself castrating—the cutting off of male life. It is at this juncture that psychoanalysis understands castration as both essential and tragic. Castration becomes not only a concrete fear but a symbolic one, and it is picked up as such in a boy's internal, nonverbal perception. The father's motivation is defense of his own life, understood symbolically as his phallic power. If the boy successfully defies the father—as his urgings and desire prompt him to do—and remains attached to the mother, he is seduced into remaining a factor of her domain, her son-lover. There would seem to be no way for a son to develop as a man without undergoing oedipal erotic defeat, thus castration. This is a Freudian insight of the greatest importance in masculine development.

Father-threat directed toward the boy in the oedipal conflict is castration as rejection. Conversely, castration from the mother occurs through the boy's success in remaining "hers," through a kind of psychological merging with her. For Freud, the way for a boy to negotiate the oedipal situation is by means of an inner experience of castration from the father, not from the mother. When a boy wins his mother, if his libido goals are met, he is mother-castrated; when he is set aside by his father, he is father-castrated. Many nightmares of five-year-olds are expressions of this insoluble dilemma. Father-castration, however, is a necessary antecedent to masculine completion, as mother-castration is not.

Freud's understanding of the true course for an oedipal boy is a temporary defeat at the hands of his father. As the boy turns away from both father and mother, he enters the latency period, where sexual interests go underground. He becomes unruly, an intimation of the rage he will feel throughout his life when castration threat intrudes. Over the long haul of latency, a boy who accepts his father's castrating authority seeks a restoration of himself through his association with other boys. And also a subsequent reunion with his father. It is the father's task in the latency period to become a role-model for his son, to repair the terrifying wounding of castration, to encourage a surprising identification with one's former oppressor.

It is as though the boy's phallic identity were "regrown" in six long years of rowdy boyhood, often much to the consternation of his mother, teachers and church, and to the pride of his father. The libidinal aim is puberty, appropriate phallic aggressivity and the dawning of erotic desire for a female who is not his mother.

Freud taught that in the oedipal drama a father's castrating prohibition becomes introjected as superego, a generalized inner voice of fairness and conscience as well as rigidified law. The psychological basis of the superego lies in the boy's newly acquired identification with his father, and the father's rules, rather than his mother's comfort. The masculine principle (and grid) is born ontogenetically in a boy's bowing to the authority of his father through acceptance of the father's castration threat and his own imitation of the father's aggressive stance. Freud saw this dynamic as the turning point, the fulcrum upon which all subsequent masculine development depends. The presence of phallic manhood hangs upon the issue of castration and "de-castration"—the restoration of masculinity—another instance of the importance of transformation in masculine development.

In the latency years, a boy begins to overcome his hatred of his castrating father, first by finding a respect growing within himself for his father's tenacity, then by gradually identifying with the father, a phallic merger rather than a mother merger. It is noteworthy that a boy moves toward an identification with one who threatens his need for love rather than remaining with one who offers him solace and comfort, the so-called "identification with the aggressor." If the oedipal conflict is solved in the direction of masculinity for a boy, he actually has no choice. The fate of phallos, as biological opposite from mother, pushes him on, with a little help from his friends. Phallos expresses itself in a boy's love of his mother in the pre-oedipal stage, it is harshly disciplined in the castration threat which resolves the oedipal crisis, and it is restored through a boy's growing connection with his father.

The threat of annihilation implicit in father-castration has varying effects upon boys. To oversimplify, a phallically timid boy scurries for protection to his mother, a dangerous sign for future thrust and independence. For the "mid-boy," castration threat leaves him on the threshold of indecision, a part of him admiring his father's decisiveness, a part of him despising it. For the phallically strong boy, the challenge of the father is what he needs. It is a signal to him of invitation into the world of men. The family's phallic representative has sent him the code.

The consistent demand of the father that his son move away from the mother is the precondition of a son's identification with his father. A Jungian might see this process as archetypal, a pattern set so deeply within the psyche that it invariably reappears in each male's early years. The youngster must somehow get the message that masculinity is of such great value that both suffering and sacrifice are necessary for its attainment. One must be prepared to give up one's greatest desire in order to possess one's gender as a future reality.

Summary of castration in Freud's thinking

1) The unconscious is predicated as an additional system to consciousness in psychological reality.

2) Infantile sexuality, based upon innate instinctuality, is present from the beginning of life, naturally and unconsciously.

3) Each infant is innately psychologically bisexual, with both active and passive libidinal tendencies. The boy child continues, after birth, to express his bisexuality.

4) Little boys discover the pleasure of their penises at a very early age through its stimulation.

5) Boys assume that everyone has a penis, that this pleasure is a natural and universal human experience. They value it very highly. It is at the core of their validly narcissistic self-development.

6) Prohibition—usually by the mother—of the child's penis play, together with the boy's observation of the lack of a penis on females, imagined as a retribution for masturbation, is the beginning of a boy's rage at his mother.

7) Castration threat in the oedipal period is the means by which the boy's primary erotic attachment to the mother is resolved. Castration threat becomes the substantial means for the introjection of father authority, forming the basis of the superego. The boy's longing for a physical connection with the mother resurfaces in puberty as a new

phallic awareness, overtly genital, and switches its aim to a mother-surrogate, but still under the spell of castration threat.

8) The lack of a functioning castration threat at the oedipal stage, combined with a concurrent and consequential failure in bonding with the father-threatener, can result in a boy's psychological identification with the mother.

The permutations of this saga are of course endless. But one can clearly grasp the importance, for a boy's masculine development, of the father's interference in his son's oedipal love-affair with the mother. A father who is not interested in the boy's mother can quite unconsciously "hand over" the mother to the son as a relief, say, from her instinctual demands. The boy then slips into his father's place.

One might say that the father's own lack of phallic authority, his functional castration, is passed on to his son, in the sense that inadequate husbanding and fathering are a counterpart of castration. The transformation in the oedipal period from bisexuality to rooted masculinity only takes place within the context of a father-prohibition. Without the prohibition, of which castration is the implicit correlate, there is no effective transformation and, consequently, there is a weakening of the inner structure—masculine grid—upon which male self-confidence can depend.

I know of one father who took his son in hand, quite clear in his instinctual grasp of what his son needed. He took a boy of the timid type, tied through early childhood weakness to his mother, and by sheer dint of effort raised that boy to "mid-boyhood," perhaps more, as a young man. I observed a remarkable effort on the part of that father over a long period of time and saw the difference that it made to the son. He sided up to his son, engaged with him in athletics, included him in large tasks. He paid fatherly attention, aware of how dangerously close their son was to his mother. The father knew nothing of Freud's schema or any other abstract psychology. He sensed the need and worked diligently to give to his son his masculine inheritance.

The castration complex

A distinction must be made between castration anxiety and the castration complex. I am indebted to Freud for my understanding that castration anxiety is ubiquitous among men and that no firmly grounded masculinity is possible without its having been encountered and, in some way, mastered through the transformations of childhood and puberty.

The castration complex, as such, forms in a male's unconscious when an event or events take place causing a boy inwardly to perceive that something essential to his being as a male actually has been taken from him. Ever after, he has a hole, a weak spot in his masculine grid, an emptiness, where a strong rod, or a joining of rods, would seem to belong. He is perched on the edge of a precipice, and suddenly the void becomes almost tangible by what someone says or does. I once had an analysand, an accomplished attorney, who called an esteemed colleague and former boss in a distant city, to check out his working of a case. His mentor asked whether he had checked out thus and so. My analysand had not; he panicked and said that he had. He lied to a man he respected. My own applesauce story, in the introduction, is another example of a castration complex on the edge of explosion.

The castration complex functions as all complexes do, as an autonomous intrusion upon smooth ego control and continuity. The complex has a chip on its shoulder. The castration complex tends to appear whenever a man's hold upon his masculine identity is threatened and his ego stability wavers. It is as though the "castration knife" severs a line securing his self-confidence. A weakness in the masculine grid allows the complex to rise to the surface. It insinuates itself, shaking his masculine integrity. Sometimes it just plumb takes over. Then his reasonableness falls to pieces.

The castration complex has mythical power and typically produces an emotional reaction far outweighing the incident which provoked it—an inner sense of dis-ease, perhaps catastrophe and panic. The omnipresence of castration anxiety becomes a dense and substantial pocket of terror in men who carry within themselves a castration complex. An incendiary reservoir is ready to be ignited. The complex is impervious to reason and explanation, circumventing vaunted male logos (except, of course, when one is writing a book about castration). The eruption of affect makes a man ashamed; a weakness is exposed. Men who suffer from unrepaired castration and its complex bear within themselves the secret suspicion that the essence of their masculinity is weak, that they have been irreparably injured. In an unexpected moment of vulnerability, the complex is touched.

Two Freudians: Karen Horney and Heinz Kohut

Karen Horney was a German-born, Berlin-trained analyst of Protestant background, a rarity among those in the early psychoanalytic circle. She emigrated to the United States in the early 1930s and practiced and taught in Chicago. In the forties she established the Karen Horney Institute in New York.

Horney was a courageous woman, challenging Freud in some of his basic concepts early in the history of psychoanalysis. According to Harold Kelman, who wrote the introduction to *Feminine Psychology,* a volume of her essays, Horney's core concept was that creature anxiety *(Angst der Kreatur)* is a fundamental human condition, a sense of hopelessness in a fundamentally hostile world, highlighted in the neurotic avoidance of feeling. In this concept, her work makes one mindful of the viewpoint of Daseinanalysis (see chapter three).

Horney's major challenge to Freudian theory was her contention that a male's dread of the female was not a factor of the female's already-accomplished castration. A male's distrust and resentment is based upon his envy of the female's capacity to become a mother. To Horney, motherhood was central to the nature of the feminine, while penis-envy was a result of women's cultural subordination. Horney reversed the envy issue, stating that "motherhood represents a more vital problem [for men] than Freud assumes."[31] She began a shift away from Freud's phallocentrism, doing so by positing the mother,

---

[31] *Feminine Psychology,* p. 22.

rather than phallos, as the power source.

According to Horney, male dread of the vagina, therefore, is not rooted in castration anxiety—from knowing there is genitalia without penis—but rather refers back to the mystery of motherhood from which the male is excluded. She embellished her argument:

> Now one of the exigencies of the biological differences between the sexes is this—that the man is actually obliged to go on proving his manhood to the woman. There is no analogous necessity for her; even if she is frigid, she can engage in sexual intercourse and conceive and bear a child. She performs her part by merely *being,* without any *doing*—a fact that has always filled men with admiration and resentment. The man, on the other hand, has to *do* something in order to fulfill himself. The ideal of "efficiency" is a typical masculine ideal in the male-dominated western world, oriented toward the materialistic, the mechanistic, toward action based on a universe divided into subjects and objects in opposition.[32]

It is the "doing" necessity for the male that is directly related to phallos. Castration is a metaphor for a man's inability to do, and the masculine need to do explains why castration is the basic masculine threat that it is. Horney moved significantly away from Freud by characterizing the feminine as "being" rather than passivity, essentially eliminating Freud's notion of feminine masochism as the expression of a woman's guilt at not having a penis. But however much this improves upon Freud in understanding the feminine psyche, it only deepens the issue of castration for men.

Horney also made a suggestion that I half resent her making, since the notion occurred to me in the midst of an analytic session some years ago, and I had been gloriously nursing the possibility that it was original. She stated that the anatomical-psychological nucleus of castration fear in men lies in the fact that during intercourse the male entrusts his genitalia to a woman's body.

> [He] presents her with his semen and interprets this as a surrender of vital strength to the woman, similar to his experiencing the subsid-

---

[32] Ibid., p. 30.

ing of erection after intercourse as evidence of having been weakened by the woman.[33]

My own fantasy was that castration was suggested to males since the dawning of consciousness by the firm and directed way phallos enters the female body in the heat of passion, and the spent and depleted way it leaves after climax. Phallos enters alive; it leaves in a manner suggesting death. Horney connected this analogue of death to a man's longing for the mother, who archetypally brings both life and death as aspects of her presence.

In a brilliant example of psychoanalytical paradoxical thinking, Horney speculated further that castration anxiety is actually a man's ego response to an unconscious wish to *be* a woman, a suggestion so outrageous to phallos that it makes one stop to wonder if there may be something to it. At this point, Horney turned the tables on Freud, using Freud's own notion of unconscious motivation to suggest the feminine as fundamental. It is axiomatic in psychoanalytic thinking that what one fears greatly is desired by an unconscious part of oneself.

Heinz Kohut, who died in 1981, was medically trained in Vienna and analytically trained in Chicago, where he taught for many years. His major works, *The Analysis of the Self* and *The Restoration of the Self,* have been instrumental in the formation of a subgroup within psychoanalysis called Self-Psychology. Kohut's central thesis, in the words of Joel Kovel, is that "narcissism is a whole separate line of development to be set alongside the sexual instincts, and that the outcome of healthy narcissism is the formation of a stable, integrated mature Self."[34]

According to Kohut, the young child finds its validity mirrored in "self-objects" which carry the inner reality of life, and which, if positive, are marked by an empathy which affirms the child's existence. The need for self-objects never ends. Kovel calls Kohut's point of

---

[33] Ibid., pp. 116-117.
[34] *The Age of Desire: Reflections of a Radical Psychoanalyst,* p. 265.

view, "raising narcissism to the level of a force of nature."[35]

To me, Kohut's self-object concept seems to move in the direction of Jung's transpersonal Self—as regulating center of the psyche—that is, toward religious awareness. However, a self-object appears to me to be the product of primitive projection, since Kohut does not differentiate between the self as an element in the process of ego formation and the Self as an inner objective "Thou." The self-object is real and the ego is formed in relationship to it, rather than the ego being a limited incarnation of the Self, as for Jung.

In his essay, "The Reexamination of Castration Anxiety," Kohut moves castration from a source-point of male fear, as it was for Freud, to a secondary, reactive position, a symptom rather than a cause. "A disorder of the self—the basic disease . . . causes the castration anxiety,"[36] a product of "the cause-and-effect sequence of self-object failure and defect in the structure of the self."[37] Therefore,

> The self psychological observer, focusing not only on the phenomenon but also on the milieu (i.e., the child's self-object environment) in which the phenomenon arose, will not view castration anxiety as a feature of the oedipal phase of the healthy child of healthy parents.[38]

From the standpoint of castration, Kohut is interesting primarily because he makes heroic efforts to connect anxiety over the loss of masculinity to an insufficiency of the ego as perceived in the child's self-object. Such an argument clearly moves away from Freud's instinct theories in the direction of emphasizing the cultural determinants of personality, but it does little to illuminate why it is that a secure possession of masculine gender symbolization is so important to men. Castration is used in Kohut's essay to illustrate his self-object theory and not to illuminate problems of masculine identity per se.

---

[35] Ibid., p. 267.
[36] *How Does Analysis Cure?*, p. 13.
[37] Ibid., p. 14.
[38] Ibid.

In closing this section, I want to highlight a remarkable statement of Freud's at the end of his life:

> Two themes come into especial prominence and give the analyst an unusual amount of trouble. It soon becomes evident that a general principle is at work here . . . tied to the distinction between the sexes . . . . [and] there is an obvious correspondence between them. . . . The two corresponding themes are in the female, *an envy for the penis*—a positive striving to possess a male genital—and in the male, *a struggle against his passive or feminine attitude toward another male* [italics added]. What is common to the two themes was singled out at an early date by psycho-analytic nomenclature as an attitude toward the castration complex. . . . I think that, from the start, "repudiation of femininity" would have been the correct description of this remarkable feature in the psychical life of human beings. . . . We often have the impression that with the wish for a penis and the masculine protest we have penetrated through all the psychological strata and have reached *bedrock* [italics added], and that thus our activities are at an end.[39]

The "repudiation of femininity" together with "a struggle against his passive or feminine attitude toward another male" sum up for Freud, at the end of his long career, the personal effort a man must make if he is not to regress into passivity or femininity, which Freud considered to be contraindications of masculinity.

I want to leave the reader at this point with that thought clearly in mind. Freud put his finger on a basic problem for men that can hardly be denied. It forms the underlayer against which the transformations mentioned in chapter one are the antithesis. One must grasp the enormous power of the feminine attributed by Freud and Jung to the unconscious to understand the emergence of patriarchal domination in the outer world as a compensation. Freud might have used "differentiation from" rather than "repudiation of" with regard to the feminine, but that is straining at gnats. Freud's words express the crucial necessity for a man not to be feminine, to stand for who he is rather than who his mother wants him to be.

---

[39] "Analysis Terminable and Interminable," *Complete Works*, vol. 23, pp. 250-252.

Freud wrote: "It may well be that nothing of considerable importance can occur in the organism without contributing to the excitation of the sexual instinct."[40] Since biology was seen by Freud as the primary influence in life, this statement alerts one to the implications of biological primacy, however obscured, in quite ordinary situations. Jung understood the importance of biology, but chaffed at its limitation as a final explanation of psyche. Freud's viewpoint deeply disturbed him and he rejected "the reductive causalism of his whole outlook, and the almost complete disregard of the teleological directedness which is so characteristic of everything psychic."[41]

Withal, biology, as the animal world tells us, is the first line of defence against nonbeing. Freud, in positing a biological foundation for psyche, erred not in starting at that point, but ending there as well. Jung, exasperated at such confinement, pressed toward meaning. While sexuality was the issue for Freud, the *numinosity* of sexuality was the issue for Jung. Jung's curiosity was focused on "teleological directedness." If sexuality is so pervasive as to be present even in childhood, what does its presence indicate about the meaning of life for everyone?

C.G. Jung

Jung's view of psychology was not developmental, in the sense that developmental psychology understands psyche to be a product of one's personal history and environment. Jung had no specific goals about what a person's life should be, no "line of development," as Freud did. Jung's approach was circular, symbolic and feminine, even as Freud's was linear, rational and masculine.

The difference might be summarized by envisioning an imaginary parent who communicates to a child as Freud: "This is the pattern of life. Grow up in accordance with it." Or as Jung: "Life has many

---

[40] "Three Essays on the Theory of Sexuality" (II. Infantile Sexuality), ibid., vol. 7, p. 205.
[41] *Symbols of Transformation,* CW 5, p. xxiii.

patterns. Find yours and grow up in accordance with it." To this day, followers of Freud and Jung exhibit this attitudinal difference, though few would suggest that either position ever totally excludes the other.

Jung was fascinated with the outcast, one who was not able to fit into an expected, or as Jung expressed it, collective, mold. He spent much of his life reading the literature of the "odd" person who saw and knew something that escaped those who were "well adjusted." When one reads Freud's seemingly endless ruminations on the psychological implications of, for example, "looking," as in the importance of scatology,[42] one connects with Jung's exasperation at Freud's "reductive causalism."

Reductive causalism has set a tone that characterizes developmental psychology to this day, with its fascination for cracks in the mirror one looks into, double looking, reflections on looking, errors in looking, abstractions (and abstracts) on looking, proofs of looking, disputations concerning looking, ontological looking and the intersubjectivity of looking. Jung's interest in looking was to find out what the odd person saw.

Jung cared little about the metaphysics of abstraction. His tireless search in cultural history for corollaries to the odd person's odd vision stamps Jung himself as an outcast in an empirical world of linguistics. His etymological meanderings were in pursuit of story, of the amplification of word-sounds, of emotion. Jung loved the feminine. He was a romantic. His psychological rootage was deeply agrarian, primitive and peasant, however sophisticated his education. He assumed, as all natural people do, that if one sees something, it must, in some way, be there. The mountain man knows mystery embedded in the natural order.

For Jung, in the words of Stephen Jay Gould, "only [the] adult arrangement matters."[43] Classical Jungians retain this orientation, a point of view in stark contrast with that of Freud and his successors

---

[42] See "Three Essays on the Theory of Sexuality," *Complete Works,* vol. 7.
[43] *Ontogeny and Phylogeny,* p. 162.

in developmental psychology. Personally I find it necessary to understand Freud's work in the area of masculine development and then to build upon it in Jung's mythic and prospective direction. In therapy, as well as in human relationships in general, it is crucial to touch the preverbal place of early childhood feeling if healing is to take place.

If, for example, a man is suffering from severe castration anxiety stemming from the lack of his father's restorative presence in latency years, the transference relationship with the therapist must reach an emotional point permitting restoration if phallic confidence is to be appreciably restored. That is Freud. Jung's mythic addition to Freud requires the identification of that emotional point of meeting with soul, that which will enable a man bereft of personal father to come into contact with archetypal father through the mediation of the analyst. The man can then walk away from therapy born anew into his primary inheritance, however "undevelopmental" the resolution.

Jung alluded to castration more than he specifically discussed it. One does not find a theory of castration in Jung's work. He shed light on the mythological meaning of castration, the loss or non-attainment of masculinity, through the examination of ancient images. He used the artifacts of psyche rather than those of postnatal development or behavior. Here I will take a short piece of Jung's writing and use it as a springboard. This piece concerns rebirth, and it becomes for me an illustration of what I call the final masculine transformation of individuation.

The hero

In *Symbols of Transformation,* Jung explored the archetypal motif of the hero's birth and rebirth.[44] The hero has a natural origin like anyone else, but he also has a second beginning, a spiritual awakening, a confirmation of his more-than-ordinary status, an "undevelopmental" aspect.

For Jung, the hero is an archetypal image which displays essential elements of what a man might become. The hero also stands in a

---

[44] "The Dual Mother," CW 5, pars. 464-612.

larger context as the prototype of ego consciousness, even of ego itself. Jung was not specifically interested in masculinity; he assumed it. That he equated ego consciousness with the hero/masculine archetype is indicative of Jung's assumption that masculinity was the standard by which one understands ego consciousness. In this regard he was not unlike Freud; both were products of a patriarchal culture. In equating hero with ego, Jung had in mind the difficulty inherent in the human situation of moving out of a childish relationship to one's original matrix. Here, however, I focus upon the hero as a masculine image, rather than a human ideal.

Jung radically questioned "collective dominants," as he called traditional—I would say patriarchal—assumptions, greatly valuing the (maternal) unconscious. Freud tended to do the opposite. In my estimation, there is a validity in using the image of the young, risk-taking hero as a model for the dawning of ego consciousness, which is characterized by a masculine, penetrating, yang mode of activity. Jung understood yin consciousness—natural, receptive, intuitive, nurturant, erotic—as equally real, the counterpart to aggressive ego. By means of such a differentiation one can grasp Jung's honoring of the feminine as well as the masculine.

As masculine paradigm, the hero must do battle with monsters and bad guys. He contends with all manner of Great Mother minions who hold back his progress, drawing him back into inertia. However, at the point where I begin my consideration, Jung's emphasis is on the psychological requirement for the hero to acknowledge his own participation in that against which he has heretofore battled. This is a sophisticated modulation. Paradox—the Christian admonition to love those who spitefully use one is a variation on the same theme, the integration of shadow is another—is not what one normally expects in the domain of ego consciousness. It is a radical transformation of conventional attitudes, a growing ability to comprehend that all human beings, even one's enemies, carry projective aspects of oneself. Without such knowledge, human beings are at a loss to escape from an endless round of efforts to establish themselves at the expense of others.

The hero's erotic desire for a princess is a result of projection, for the hero is not yet able to comprehend his own inner femininity. Nor should he, since the point of the heroic stance is the establishment of masculinity. One ordinarily understands the hero from that point of view. His imagistic function is to help us grasp the necessity for both masculine development and ego consciousness as a movement away from a primitive maternal origin. Without such a movement, there is no differentiated ego/hero. Everything is stuck in a kind of amorphous, hermaphroditic mass. The would-be hero is entangled with the Mother; his incipient phallos is lost in her folds. Thus the requirement for the transformations I have mentioned. The hero must discover himself as masculine and his opposite as feminine.

Projections happen because outer and inner reality mirror each other. Jung never much used the vocabulary of narcissism (as in mirroring), perhaps due to its association with Freud's autoerotic aspect of infantile sexuality. But he did insist upon the complementary function of consciousness relative to the unconscious, personal and collective, and vice versa. His emphasis on wholeness as the destiny of psyche necessitates the inclusion of the opposite—the feminine—toward which masculine development needs to evolve. Therefore, the contrary of what the hero takes as his goal is also his goal, though the hero does not know this in the heat of his labors. This is a crucial element in the movement of ego-consciousness toward a working relationship with what Jung called the Self, and fundamental in an understanding of the individuation process.

Wotan and individuation

In "The Dual Mother," Jung attempted to clarify this rather sophisticated notion. He did so, typically, in a lengthy digression, elaborating on Wagner's *Die Walküre* smack in the middle of a previous sidewinder on Longfellow's *Hiawatha*. Jung's digressions are infamous, difficult and often infuriating. They are rarely beside the point, however, no matter how torturous the process might be to one's line of attention. Jung wrote in a highly intuitive, romantic (as opposed to technological), associative vein, quite "right-brain" compared to Freud's "left-brain" mode.

Jung was sparked by the myth of Wotan and family; I am sparked by Jung's imaginings. It has been difficult for me to ascertain how closely Jung's use of the Wotan story conforms to the myth, a complicated business. It has been almost as difficult for me to be certain how Jung used the myth. Nonetheless, certain ideas used by Jung in his interpretation are seminal to me in my investigation of masculine transformation, castration and rage. Jung wrote:

> It is clear from all this that Wagner's Brünhilde is one of the numerous anima-figures who are attributed to masculine deities, and who, without exception, represent a dissociation in the masculine psyche—a "split-off" [complex] with a tendency to lead an obsessive existence of its own. This tendency to autonomy causes the anima to anticipate the thoughts and decisions of the masculine consciousness, with the result that the latter is constantly confronted with unlooked-for situations which it has apparently done nothing to provoke. Such is the situation of Wotan, and indeed of every hero who is unconscious of his own intriguing femininity. . . .
>
> Brünhilde's sin was her support of Siegmund, but behind that lies the incest which was projected into the brother-sister pair. The symbolical meaning, however, is that Wotan, the father, *has entered into his own daughter in order to rejuvenate himself.* . . . And the instrument of fate is always the woman, who knows and reveals his secret thoughts: hence the *impotent rage of Wotan*, who cannot bring himself to recognize *his own contradictory nature.*[45]

What might have been Wotan's "secret thoughts"? The desire to break the incest taboo? Might Jung, in writing of dissociation in the masculine psyche—a man's own intriguing femininity—be suggesting something similar to the Karen Horney notion mentioned earlier, that man has a "secret wish" to be a woman? Jung ordinarily represented the hero's secret thought as a desire to stop working so hard, to quit trying, to lie down and just forget about the whole thing—which would mean reentering the mother as a relief from the tough life of ordeal and sacrifice. These temptations signify a surrender of

---

[45] Ibid., pars. 563-564, italics added.

the heroic quest, and by definition the acceptance of an incomplete masculinity.

If, indeed, there is a correlation between Horney's secret wish and Jung's/Wotan's secret thoughts, we are on to something new. Jung connected the secret thoughts of Wotan, and the anima figure's knowing these, with Wotan's "impotent rage" and his need to "bring himself to recognize his own contradictory nature." Wotan's contradictory nature as "secret thought" and Horney's "secret wish" both have to do with the feminine and the extent to which femininity is a threat to phallos' primary establishment within the psychology of a man. Wotan's secret emerges as instinctual desire, a projection of a hidden part of himself onto "his own daughter."

Melanie Klein, an early Freudian, made a suggestion that appears to be relevant to this discussion in her 1928 paper, "Early Stages of the Oedipal Conflict." She wrote that "in the *femininity complex of the male,* there is at bottom the frustrated desire for a special organ."[46] In different words, Klein, Horney and Jung ("Such is the situation of Wotan, and indeed of every hero who is unconscious of his own intriguing femininity") are all referring to a similar phenomenon in masculinity, looking at it from varied perspectives. Jung saw the feminine in the masculine as an intrinsic reality, given his view of holistic individuation as the destiny of psyche. He gave the name anima—the Latin word for soul—to the "intriguing femininity" that is "split off" under the spell of ego repression in established men. Jung personally experienced his own femininity in his projections upon women, so the notion was not an abstract one to him.

Jung could not have used a more likely example of one unconscious of his inner "intriguing femininity" than Wotan. Wotan's character is archetypally phallic. He was the god of nocturnal storms. His name, according to *Larousse,* was derived "from the very word which in all Germanic languages expressed frenzy and fury (in modern German *Wuten,* to rage)."[47]

---

[46] *The Selected Melanie Klein,* p. 74, italics added.
[47] *New Larousse Encyclopedia of Mythology,* p. 253.

Wotan was the horseman in the sky in pursuit of game; he became the god who granted heroism and decided man's fate—the god of spiritual life. His associates in this work are his daughters, *die Walküre* (the Valkyries), awful and beautiful, who hover over a battlefield choosing who shall be slain. Brünhilde was a Valkyrie, and Jung made her Wotan's anima, his "instrument of fate." She "belongs to him"; the Valkyrie "is" Wotan. In a similar way, a female figure in a man's dream "is" the dreamer's anima. By emotionally connecting with the figure, a dreaming man can begin to know a part of himself which the ego might not accept were it offered straightforwardly, in a declarative manner.

The anima in Wotan comes to the fore, interrupting his classic masculine stance. She "knows and reveals his secret thoughts," exposing and expressing the feminine within, always ready to be projected without. Wotan doesn't get it, however much Jung gets it. Men, ordinarily, don't get it. It is typical that others see one's femininity long before a man sees his own, as Jung sees Wotan's. The barrier to this piece of masculine self-knowledge, crucial to individuation, is what one might call phallic defense (Alfred Adler called it "the masculine protest"), which, after a successful negotiation of the earlier transformations, has done its job and should get out of the way. If it does not get out of the way, one suspects that power needs remain necessary for a man's phallic sense of himself, that his "secret" undermines his phallic confidence.

Jung's statement—"hence, the impotent rage of Wotan"—can be seen as the leitmotif of my present work: impotence, a form of castration, juxtaposed with rage. They are counterparts of one another. In the quotation, impotence modifies rage. One does not know whether Jung intended "impotent" to be understood in a sexual sense or as a figure of speech. Either way, the source of the image is phallos energy constricted, followed immediately by rage. Wotan fears what the anima/woman reveals: his secret thought. Here is the correlation with Horney's suggestion of the "secret wish" of men; the anima in Wotan is not only his wish, she is part of him, obscured by his masculine ego. The anima whispers his own "intriguing femininity" to Wotan, which contradiction impedes potency, suggesting castration.

The first five transformations, as outlined above in chapter one, have the effect of concealing the potential hero's femininity. Were he experientially to continue his bisexual nature much beyond the oedipal struggle, were the latency period not for him a transition from very-young-boy into older-but-still-clearly-boy, and were the onset of puberty not the start of a still-older-boy-now-on-the-threshold-of-manhood transformation, we would have no hero. A boy's "intriguing femininity" must sink into dormancy in the unconscious if the classic workings out of heroic young manhood are to coalesce in his personality, what I call the masculine grid. In latency there is an inner urge to pinch the girls and make them cry. They become foreign. The girl in the boy must be distanced. It is in puberty that intimacy becomes attractive.

A danger for the hero is that he will accede to his secret thought, give in to his feminine nature, characterized by the mother, and seek solace. His energy, his phallic stamina, leaves him. He finds himself wanting to "reenter the mother" not as rebirth but as relief from the hero's tough life, to sacrifice the heroic quest rather than the mother. If the situation is examined closely, indications of identity with the mother emerge. A particular symptom is indolence, for indolence is a telling sign of a man's failed oedipal severance from his Beloved Comforter, whether or not the actual mother was in fact comforting. The inner image of mother functions psychologically with or without assistance from one's natural parent.

Here is where a knowledge of Jung's work is critical. He adds an essential archetypal dimension to Freud's concrete and personal-historical view of male identification with and longing for "mother." An older man's continuing need for comfort and indulgence bespeaks a mother problem. It can be chronically debilitating or episodic or fleeting. Every man will know that something is wrong when the mother complex is present and intruding in his life, whether or not he calls it by this name.

Wotan symbolically lies with his daughter and soothes himself with her "rejuvenating power." The psychological question is whether this is a regression to the primal mother, damaging to heroic phallos, or a movement forward to the Mother of individuation/rebirth. The need to recapture his youth is a critical peg upon which a man's direction turns. I understand Jung's point to be that it was, for Wotan, regressive, since it provoked "impotent rage." The god cannot "bring himself to recognize his own contradictory nature"; his rebirth is blocked. Wotan is engaged in a hapless slide, returning to Mama in the guise of his daughter, dazzled by the chimera of a rejuvenating power through his sexual engagement. Wotan's inability to be conscious of the dual nature of himself, full man with anima, puts him negatively into the hands of his own inner and repressive feminine. She does not take on new meaning, but actually becomes the enemy a man fears his inner femininity to be. Fulfillment in such a case gives only temporary release from the rigors required of the hero.

The message from Jung in this vignette is that men must bring themselves to recognize and accept a hidden and terrifying feminine part of themselves. The natural place for this to happen is in the transformational stage of individuation, the mid-life opportunity for rebirth, once phallic establishment is secure. An inability to do this inevitably and paradoxically works against potency. A result is rage, for it is, in its way, another form of castration. The truly new aspect of individuation potency—rebirth potency one might call it—lies in the necessity to accept one's femininity, rather than to reject it, as in the five prior transformational stages.

What might this look like in a "first-world" man's life? He might strive unrelentingly for twenty or thirty years to establish himself in business, to provide a home for his family and an education for his children, to become a respected member of his community, with admired opinions and commitments. Suddenly, it seems, his labors turn to ash. He is retired early; his wife finds her independent voice, perhaps her independent way of life; his children are unwilling to be cloned to his example. His pride in himself, his potency, vanishes, perhaps literally, almost surely metaphorically. The scenario can vary in any number of ways; his own sense of himself disintegrates in depression. He wants his old self returned. He wants rejuvenation.

Sometimes, a measure of an old, strongly phallic self can be retrieved, but with a loss of masculine transformational maturity. For a man to become wise in his old age, there is no substitute for an embrace, within himself, of his opposite, his own femininity, his softness, his relatedness—in a sense, his phallic defeat. The effort to regain his younger phallic surety is what Jung calls "the regressive restoration of persona," the pseudo-accomplishment of a bygone youthfulness with its rock-hard, seemingly uncomplicated erections. For a man to grow old well, he must accept the need for this last transformation within himself, a reversal of projection of his feminine upon the women in his life. A gentleness emerges from within, a willingness to work within the container, to allow being, without forcing life into a unilateral phallic mode.

The inner need for rejuvenation, urged on by instinct and fantasized through sexual connection, is simultaneously both physical and spiritual. In the earlier transformations, instinct is clearly in charge, even when it modulates into accomplishment. In the individuation years, sexual yearning suggests a man's need for something more than obtaining an outer object of desire. Sexual desire is always a powerful merging of the currents of psyche and physis, whether a man is young or old. If, in the mature man, the language of sexual desire is only infantile/adolescent—for surely it is always infantile/adolescent in *some* part of itself, and that is why it is archetypally rejuvenating—the inner mixture of masculinity and femininity is never discovered.

Jung believed that a man—specifically, the heroic ego in a man—must make two sacrifices before the transformation of individuation can occur. One has to do with a childish longing for the past; more especially, longing for the mother and the comfort and security she represents. The other is an adult pride in one's accomplishment, without which sacrifice the man will stay where he is and never move beyond it.

Freud did not much use the word sacrifice. But over and again in his writings there is insistence that masculine development takes place through detachment, abandonment, surrender, renunciation, all synonyms for the sacrifice of infantile gratification. For Freud, since his emphasis was on childhood sexuality, the issue is focused in the oedipal separation from the mother, in early and predispositional impediments to maturity. For Jung, the establishment of an accomplished ego is but the first part of psychological maturity. Amazingly, he saw that this, too, must be surrendered, in the second sacrifice. The alternative to a sacrifice of ego accomplishment is that, in Jung's words: "Everything young grows old, all beauty fades, all heat cools, all brightness dims, and every truth becomes stale and trite."[48]

What does it mean to integrate the feminine?

There is always the danger, in proposing some aspects of feminine integration, that my list might be skewed by stereotypical notions of the feminine, established by, or in reaction against, dominant patriarchal conceptions. My intention, however, is to seek out whatever archetypal core might lie beneath the patriarchal tradition. As discussed in chapter one, beneath the contorted surface of the stereotype lies a nugget of archetypal pattern, however much distortion might occur in cultural and familial transmission.

My notion of what integration of the feminine might involve, without danger to phallos, looks something like this, briefly, impressionistically and somewhat unevenly sketched:

1) Feeling

A man must begin to know that he has feeling and that an inner sense of who and where he is matters to him. I use feeling here in the Jungian sense, as the capacity to value, rather than emotionality. A man's growing consciousness of himself as an interior being, rather than exterior only, is the point. The French *sentiment* is what is meant, not the English "sentimentality." The Jungian nuance, value, is an interior inclination, which is what makes feeling so typically

---

[48] *Symbols of Transformation*, CW 5, par. 553.

difficult for a man. It is perspective, temper of mind (as mood rather than product), disposition. One man found it a revelation that he was attending to his feeling when he spent long hours, days, even years in an introspective wondering, an attitude of attention to questions of meaning in his personal life. This is introverted feeling.

Once a friend of mine, living very far from his exwife and sons and very busy in his vocation and thoughtfully involved in the issues of his fate told me that his older son was graduating from high school. "You're going, of course," I said. He hadn't seriously thought of doing so. He was a man, at that point, out of touch with the value to him of his son, to say nothing of what might be his son's sense of need for him. Cogency and accomplishment came first to this man. He was masculinely extraverted, but extraverted *feeling,* connection with another, was out of range for him.

2) Emotion

Emotionality, the expression of intense reaction to an awareness of feeling, is considered by males to be so stereotypically feminine that they commonly give affective behavior no significant room in their psychological houses. The only time I ever saw my father shed a tear, for example, was at his mother's burial. I will never forget his grief. I had no idea that my father was emotionally attached to her or to anyone else.

What might have happened if my father had expressed more emotion in earlier years? For one, he might have stayed at the dinner table during inevitable family squabbles, rather than silently leaving to read his paper. He might have said, "I can't stand this constant arguing!" or "Stop it, all of you!" or "Don't do that to your sister!" Instead, he walked away. He must have hated the bickering, but he never engaged his hatred, never expressed it or used it to lead. The result was that his wife and his children were left without any image of manly emotion. The effect of his disapproval was passive rather than active, and felt more rejecting than an outburst of emotion would have.

Conventional wisdom lets women express themselves, while men think, abstract, plan, organize, support. For men to get emotional is ordinarily seen as an abandonment of masculine strength and directedness. Sometimes that is the case, as when a complex seizes a man and he flies apart. But it need not be so. Men can learn to overcome the cultural restraint inhibiting emotional expression, to subjectively discover value and to express the emotion that inevitably flows from feeling. An integrated anima shows in a man's ability to recognize the strength of his personal feeling.

In Ken Burns' documentary *The Civil War*, this letter is read from Major Sullivan Ballou to his wife Sarah:

> I have, I know, but few and small claims upon Divine Providence, but something whispers to me—perhaps it is the wafted prayer of my little Edgar, that I shall return to my loved ones unharmed. If I do not my dear Sarah, never forget how much I love you, and when my last breath escapes me on the battle field, it will whisper your name. Forgive my many faults, and the many pains I have caused you. How thoughtless and foolish I have often times been! How gladly would I wash out with my tears every little spot upon your happiness....
>
> But, O Sarah! If the dead can come back to this earth and flit unseen around those they loved, I shall always be near you; in the gladdest days and in the darkest nights . . . always, always, and if there be a soft breeze upon your cheek, it shall be my breath, as the cool air fans your throbbing temple, it shall be my spirit passing by. Sarah do not mourn me dead: think I am gone and wait for thee, for we shall meet again.[49]

Major Ballou was killed within the week at Bull Run. The intensity of his love, his ownership of that love and his openness to expressing it poetically are able to move one a century and a half later.

3) Sensibility

Sensibility is refinement. Men often make it their business to be ignorant in aesthetics; they consider it unmanly to be sensitive, and, even more so, to move from sensitiveness into the grace of refinement. Men often find crudeness quite a felicitous condition, substan-

---

[49] Episode One; see also *People Magazine,* Oct. 15, 1990, p. 67.

tiating their phallic prowess. A man can live through his woman what he dares not, or can not, express for himself.

It may be that men's rejection of sensibility has its source in the necessary rejection by a boy of his mother's expectations. Her desire for her son to be "nice," not rowdy, sets the stage for a defiance from which a man might never emerge, to his own impoverishment. Aesthetic sensibility in a man, an appreciation of fineness, an at-homeness with mood, requires an extension of his personality beyond phallic establishment. He must allow himself to enter what to the rough masculine is a foreign realm, where moon rather than sun is pervasive, where impression and attitude dominate facts.

What I am calling "sensibility" here is perhaps similar to archetypal feminine brooding, the capacity to reflect on the mystery of inner generation, an experience worlds apart from male ejaculation.[50] The feminine seals off, is impervious; it gestates, grows the life within. When a man begins to feel the feminine quality of his soul, he also gains some distance from the turbulence of outer events. A certain quality of tone grows within him.

4) Relatedness

It is amazing how many men have no close friends, particularly no close men friends. By close I mean another person with whom one can talk openly and honestly about oneself, where fear of losing face (read phallos) is not an issue. Whether or not relationships of this kind are archetypally feminine in psychological nuance (I suspect that they are), certainly they are stereotypically feminine, and that is enough to put them on the suspicious list for most men. I remember my shock and disappointment after I proposed friendship, when my own phallic guard was down, to a fellow American husband and father, a banker, in Zurich. He absolutely refused, without a second thought. My suggestion was out of line in his world.

---

[50] Camille Paglia writes: "The pregnant woman is . . . complete. Brooding for nine months upon her own creation, she needs nothing and no one." (*Sexual Personae: Art and Decadence from Nefertiti to Emily Dickenson*, p. 12)

Perhaps he feared that I was leading up to some kind of physical intimacy. My wife had four women with whom she could talk seriously, openly, honestly. I had no man confidant and I wanted one, particularly one out of my own professional field. The situation in the ensuing fourteen years in the United States has not been much different. Men are wary of closeness with other men. The fear of castration and its implications is an enormous barrier.

5) Vulnerability

The female sexual organs receive those of the male. To be vulnerable means to be receptive, open to being hurt, to let one's protective barriers down. Men tend to guard themselves at every turn against intrusion, partly because their sexual organs are exposed, partly because being entered, or being available to entrance—being vulnerable—computes psychologically as being feminine, an echo of Freud's notion of the male requirement for a "repudiation of femininity." To males, vulnerability suggests passivity and receptivity. The masculine ideal is to be strong and adequately defended. Exposure of phallos and testes is already dangerous. Even more so is invasion.

True manly courage takes vulnerability into account. It is over against a man's vulnerability that courage has point; a man knows that his masculine status is at stake. He risks nonetheless because he also knows that masculinity, per se, must be proven. To accept one's vulnerability portends the end of bravado. It is a sign that a man's inner phallic structure is sufficiently in place and that he does not need to prove its presence.

I know a man in his forties who has long been a powerhouse in his community, tall, athletic, commanding, head of a large corporation. He left his marriage for apparently important reasons, but in the wake of his departure, his teenage children found themselves consumed with reaction against his long domination of the family scene and then his departure from it. The father attempted to stem the tide of disintegration through traditional leadership and heroic undertakings, but made small progress. Gradually he is learning that he cannot demand obedience or secure a certain result in his children's progress. He says, "I just can't do it any more. I can't make it happen." He realizes his loss, but stands on the threshold of another transformation. As he discovers the power his children have over his ego intentions, he feels hurt, intruded upon, surprisingly vulnerable. He is called upon to muster up another dimension of courage.

6) Weakness

It is humiliating to a man to be considered weak, the obverse of the hardness and intrepidness of phallos. For a man to come to terms with, to accept, his weakness as a person and as a man, is a genuine psychological accomplishment. Weakness, and a knowledge of one's dependence upon factors other than one's ego intentions, are correlative ideas and make a man feel that he is perilously close to falling into the foreign "feminine" realm when contrasted with phallic determination, male physical strength, male separation from childbearing and its vicissitudes. Weakness is a human element that is excised from masculine definition in the earlier transformations. In individuation, it is readmitted.

When a man says, as one of my analysands in his late forties recently did, "I'm beginning to think that it's okay for a man to be weak," he confesses movement beyond the curse of phallic fragility. He also moves toward participation in the created order as an equal, neither superior nor inferior. The emergence of weakness as a permitted masculine attribute depends upon a man's integrated awareness that he stands as one among a world of interdependent persons and that his insecurity is not a neurosis or a blight, but a part of his participation in humanity's lot. A new appreciation for women, who bear the mystery and misery of his seed and his pleasure, and a tentative and unaccustomed empathy with them begin to dawn.

7) Homoeroticism

For a man to admit that he loves another man is difficult because it implies homosexuality, and homosexuality implies that the secret inner femininity a man fears has a hold on him. For a man deeply to encounter his femininity almost inevitably involves the emergence of loving and potentially erotic feelings about men who are important to him. The feminine in the male—the anima—is attracted to the sensuality of the male friend. For a man with an established and secure phallic identity, this discovery will almost certainly come as a shock, and one that he resists.

One of the amazing and touching aspects of the AIDS epidemic, particularly as it involves the infection of homosexuals, is the extent to which an understanding, even a sympathy, has emerged in many men for the plight of their afflicted brothers. Something quite revolutionary is occurring that is difficult to identify precisely, yet one can sense it in the look in a man's eye when he hears of a neighbor falling ill, or the son of a friend nearing the end. Is it a "there but for the grace of God . . ." reaction? If so, consciousness is in a different place from where it was before the scourge began.

8) Feminism

A man feeling the impact of individuation begins to understand that women have suffered under the domination of patriarchal social structures and collective norms. His social ideas change. The individuating man, in integrating his feminine, will find a widening gap between himself and men who unquestioningly claim their supposedly superior position toward everything feminine. Or behave as though they do, whether or not they obviously claim it. It occurs to such a man that a relegation of the feminine to an inferior role implicates a part of himself.

There is a collective implication in individuation. The feminine as "subjective" is no longer as foreign as it was. A woman telling a man that she objects to one or another—or a raft—of his presumptuous directives no longer comes across simply as threat. He can take it. He can listen. How difficult it is for a man to be silent, to listen and to process what he hears! His leadership program has not prepared him for this. Once he gets the drift, a man might actually discover that he wants to hear what his woman, his children, his associates, have to say. He tires of unilateral leadership; the anima speaks to him inwardly and encourages him to loosen up, to engage himself in the pleasure of learning from one who beforehand, or even presently, might be oppositional. Taking in, which surely has a feminine implication, comes as a relief from always giving out.

9) *Tenderness*

To be tender suggests softness, which in turn suggests femininity. Tenderness is scorned by boys who need to experience a chasm between themselves and their mothers during latency, and it remains a feminine-aversive personality trait throughout the lives of males generally. Men make a virtue of being tough. Being tender tends to be equated with being soft-headed, a loser.

Tenderness, however, is a remarkable place where the masculine and the feminine meet in a physical—and psychological—congruence. A man is not without his tender parts; the exquisite excitability of his sexual organs, especially, is a clue to a man, if he will listen to his body. The omnipresence of castration fear in males circumambulates the extraordinary value males place on the actual and symbolic importance of their sexuality, which finds its epitome in physical tenderness. The unblocking of body awareness in men goes hand in hand with a growing appreciation for, and subjective knowledge of, the feminine. Men who are conscious of the castration injury they have suffered tend to be men who have experienced their own tenderness. Their task is to translate their shame into an honoring of their wound.

In her novel of prehistoric Alaskans, Sue Harrison writes of the destruction of Chagak's village and her people by an invading tribe. In a new settlement, Chagak was raped and impregnated by a warrior. Raising her child alone, she was terrified of further masculine contact, even of Kayugh, a widower with a child of his own, a man who himself had been torn asunder by war. He quietly loved her and bode his time. Finally she accepted him.

> Chagak leaned away from Kayugh's chest and looked up into his eyes. "Samiq's [her son] father hurt me," she said softly, and she saw the surprise in his face, then the anger.
> ... "I will not hurt you, Chagak," he said. He pressed her to his chest, the warmth of his skin hot against Chagak's breasts.
> ... There was a shivering inside of Chagak, something pulling

her to him, but the fear was still there, and in the darkness Chagak reached out to touch his face, as if to assure herself that it was Kayugh who was with her, Kayugh who touched her.

. . . And when Kayugh finally moved over her, lying his full length upon her, Chagak was not afraid.[51]

10) Suffering

I have heard the story that once in a seminar Jung was asked what the woman's counterpart to the hero's journey might be. Jung is said to have drawn on his pipe for a long time and then said, "Suffering."

The prototype of feminine suffering is childbirth, whether or not a woman actually bears children. The subordination of oneself to the child within—whether actual or symbolic—is archetypally feminine. There is no male equivalent to this demand of nature. Castration, however, is a masculine parallel, but at a far reach. Suffering comes to a woman through the living of her nature; castration for a man thus brings with it the implication of feminine experience. For a man to embrace suffering consciously moves him in the direction of the archetypal other, toward a reunion with the feminine on the far side of phallic attainment. The issue grows in importance as a man moves toward the end of his life.

To be male often means not to suffer oneself but to make someone else suffer, as a blatant demonstration of masculine strength. The roots of dysfunctional male aggression, perhaps even functional and essential aggression, may lie in the castration suffering a boy undergoes in the oedipal stage of transformation, with a subsequent identification with the father-aggressor taking form in his masculine grid. For a man to consciously move beyond phallic aggression—his hallmark in earlier years—requires ego cooperation with Heraclitus' psychic law of enantiodromia, "the emergence of the unconscious opposite in the course of time," as Jung expressed it.[52] Either a man embraces suffering, or suffering will overtake him.

During ritual circumcision of boys at puberty in Uganda (when I

---

[51] *Mother Earth, Father Sky,* pp. 308-309.
[52] "Definitions," *Psychological Types,* CW 6, par. 709.

lived there in 1961), the slightest indication of suffering shown meant that the ordeal had failed. Such a trial is archetypally masculine and psychologically appropriate for boys, who must learn how to be brave men. But for one entering the gate of individuation, responding to an inner press for reunion, signs of suffering indicate the approach of the portals of wholeness, of a developed humanity. Suffering is beyond masculine proving.

11) "Female" work

Attending to child care, cooking and serving meals, laundry, household maintenance, shopping, planning and management of entertaining are stereotypically relegated to women. Traditionally, it is a woman's responsibility to relieve men of these necessities.

I remember well the sense of accomplishment that came to me during one of my training sojourns in Zurich when I no longer felt nervous as passers-by stared and whispered at my hanging of laundry on our outside clothesline. Today one sees men in the supermarkets in Zurich, but still rarely in the laundry room. It is quite lovely to see strikingly masculine men in New York unselfconsciously trekking to the laundromat with babies strapped to their backs. To do culturally designated female work without embarrassment, a man must move beyond cultural expectations, beyond the caution appropriate to an earlier acceptance of role. He must know that he is doing "women's work" and that it doesn't matter.

I recently had dinner with an older male friend who'd invited two younger women to join us. On my arrival, he suggested that we have "a good stiff [that is, masculine] drink" before they came, since one woman drank no alcohol and the other only a small amount of white wine.

I accepted his offer in the spirit of male camaraderie. Yet I noticed his extraordinary preparations for the evening, the attention he paid to cooking, the many touches of elegance and care. Was my friend, the product of another time, as am I, bolstering his macho image by the offer of a stiff drink? Was he unconsciously compensating for enjoying the time he'd spent in "eros" activities?

12) Soul

Soul (anima) suggests a natural connection with the unconscious, which, because of feminine interiority, men have tended to make the preserve of the opposite sex. Men take pride in what they consider to be their left-brain attributes. The awakening of an awareness of an inner life in a man places him in a strange and unaccustomed position. He must begin to use and trust faculties that are new, that feel foreign.

Soul is per force an acknowledgment that facts are not intrinsically superior to other ways of knowing, that reason—logos in traditional and Jungian terms—is one-sided, incomplete. Anima is often negatively interpreted by persons unfamiliar with the depth of Jung's use of that term. An "anima attack" or "anima possession" will skew a man's self-control; the anima is strange, dark, foreign. Anima, as such, however, is as essential a part of male definition as is phallos. Where phallos is obvious, anima is covert, hidden, held-back and subtle, protected and obscured by husband ego.

An extraordinarily accomplished professional person, well into mid-life, recently told me he was becoming impatient with his well-managed masculine responsibilities. He had carried husbanding, fathering, earning, building and leading for a long time. He was aware of another factor in himself on the edge of emergence. This man will not throw over his duties; he is much too finely honed for that. But he is feeling a certain fatigue and boredom, a desire to experience himself somehow—he doesn't quite know—differently. In such a way does the anima appear in an established man—in moods slightly in opposition to himself, oblique, implicatory.

These are a few of the factors necessarily left behind in the first five masculine transformations. They strangely, and often uncomfortably, re-present themselves in the masculine individuation process. Without a laundry list of possibilities, the danger is that the idea of feminine integration will sound reasonable enough, even to a man, while a sense of what is entailed in living it out remains elusive. If the issue remains stuck in the intellect, change, in the final paradoxical transformation, never really takes place.

With this discussion I have anticipated the final chapter of this work, jumping over the difficulties in a male's experience of castration, and the faulted defense of his masculinity, his explosions of rage. There is need now to return to the elements of the process. A castrated man cannot enter into the *hieros gamos;* he will have no masculinity to present to his inner feminine.

3
Castration and Male Rage

In this chapter I will discuss castration anxiety, and the rage it provokes in men, under six conditions.

The first is the castration of one male by another. The second is castration inflicted by a female, commonly and unconsciously perceived by the male to be a mother-figure, whether she be, indeed, mother, or wife, lover, daughter or any other female. Both of these have already been mentioned in this work. Third is a man's castration of himself, the result of his guilt for having exercised his phallic nature in a way that appears to him to be unlawful or in some other way forbidden. Fourthly, there is societal castration: men destroyed by patriarchal structures that are oriented around dominance and submission. The fifth castration is an imposition of fate, a decision of the gods, a hostile contrivance of circumstance. And finally, there can occur what I call ontological castration, where a man's very being is called into question, where the meaning of his existence, his deepest sense of himself, is denied.

Distinctions between these categories are not always clear, nor are they immune from overlapping, as is the case in all archetypally oriented experiences.

It is noted here that depleted or undeveloped masculinity does not equal femininity, as such. Femininity is not the absence or injury of masculinity; it is a psychological characteristic in itself, the source-image of which derives from the female body. The etiological and psychological foundation of what we understand as masculinity and femininity is inextricably related to the biological differences between male and female reproductive organs and other gender-specific physical characteristics. Without such a starting point psychological talk about masculinity and femininity is meaningless. At the same time, one must be careful to acknowledge that all human beings, whether male or female, have characteristics archetypally derived from opposite-gender factors within their personalities.

This is what Freud refers to as our biological and psychological bisexuality, and what Jung calls the contrasexual component in each individual psyche. Freud's emphasis on instinct predisposed him to see castration as a man's "passive or feminine attitude toward another male."[53] He understood that castration introduced the specter of femininity in a man's psyche by undermining his sense of himself as masculine. As I see it, the deeply rooted reality of gender-opposition in the unconscious, together with both the necessity and difficulty of negotiating the various masculine transformations, conspire to produce much the same effect. The characteristics of the opposite sex are implied.

Freud's equation of passivity and the feminine attitude is a classical patriarchal notion. The two terms cannot in fact be so easily exchanged, and by quoting Freud I do not thereby indicate that I agree with him. The feminine attitude involves much more than passivity, as outlined in the previous chapter. What Freud might have said was "receptivity"; he might have talked of passivity in a man without connecting it with femininity. He did not, of course, and that causes a problem for anyone using his castration concept. For me, the peril of unwittingly falling into patriarchal thinking is an especially serious matter, since I see phallos as the alternative to masculine dependence on patriarchy.

Male-Male Castration

Freud wrote of male-male castration near the end of his life, in the famous and lengthy passage already quoted.[54] A portion of it is repeated here:

> A general principle is at work ... in the male, a struggle against his passive or feminine attitude toward another male.... "Repudiation

---

[53] See above, p. 54.
[54] Ibid.

of femininity" [is] the correct description of this remarkable feature in the psychical life of human beings.

Freud's general principle is the psychological necessity for a male to repress his femininity, his passive attitude toward other men. Horney suggested that males have a secret wish to be feminine. Jung prescribed the work and trials of the hero as the antidote to passive masculinity; he saw the danger as a falling into the mother-complex instead of facing his arduous tasks. All three addressed a similar archetypal necessity. From the Freudian viewpoint, passivity as a characteristic feature of a male's personality is a failure of (and in) the oedipal crisis. For Horney, giving in to his unconscious wish undercuts a male's gender identity. The Jungian view is that passivity is a failure in the hero's struggle for masculine establishment.

I choose to focus on Freud's designation. It has the advantage of being starkly graphic. Castration elicits an immediate emotional response from men, who understand its implication at once. It is an in-the-body image that radiates into every nook and cranny of a man's awareness. It has passed from Freud into the common speech of our time, however vaguely it is understood. The point of castration, and the usefulness of the term, is the loss of masculinity and failed masculine transformation. And the illusion of implied femininity.

An analysand told me that at the age of six or seven, his father took him for a winter hike in the mountains. There was snow on the ground. The boy was walking ahead of his father along the trail. The father stopped to urinate, then called for his son to return to where he was. When the son did so, the father pointed to the words he had spelled in the snow with his urine: "George is a baby."

This remark was the father's way of castrating his son. One might surmise that this episode was, indeed, part of the functional castration threat a father puts upon his son in the oedipal struggle. But this insult was not a father's pushing his son away from his wife in aid of securing the wife for himself and securing his son as a member of the masculine community. The act was aggressively hostile and belittling. The son instantly recognized it to be so and has carried the burden of his father's ridicule ever since. The father's action continues to register: "My father calls me a baby. Therefore, I must be a baby. He does not like me." The adult man's head knows differently, but his masculine grid carries the wound. It may be that this father's shooting down his young son was a neurotic compensation for his own failure in attaining manhood. The father, in effect, says in his snow words, "If I don't have it, you won't have it either." He is afraid of his son's potential. If the son became a man he might surpass the father. Fashioning failure as an inner reality for his son, the father passes on his own castration.

Men commonly cut each other down in social relationships, business, sports, academics, romance. Competition is a classic factor of masculine interaction. In terms of this work, cutting down is tantamount to cutting off. The aggressive nature of phallos, when active between men, makes itself felt in the insecurity men experience when they become even tacit rivals. Omnipresent male competition is reflected in a derivative word commonly used to suggest masculine attainment: competence. For one male to succeed in making another look incompetent creates the impression that he has won the battle for supremacy.

Recall the debates in the American presidential elections of 1980 and 1988. In 1980, Reagan took the initiative and held it against Carter by exclaiming with a twinkle, "There, he's doing it again!"—whatever Carter said—creating the impression that Carter was fumbling and inept. It was a masterful tactic; there was no way to defend against it. Bush similarly led out in his debates with Dukakis, enfeebling his opponent by "demonstrating" that pro-environment Dukakis could not even clean his own Boston harbor. Bush, declared by many to be a "wimp" candidate, turned the tables on the strong man and made him appear to be the impotent one.

In the 1989 film *Mississippi Burning*, castration is not left to the imagination. The fading power of the small-town white male establishment finds revenge in the castration of a black youth. The savagery serves as an intimidation to the entire black community and to the FBI, investigating the murder of three civil rights workers. At their wits' end, the FBI agents retaliate, kidnapping the mayor and threatening him with the same castration he and his cohorts wreaked upon the youth.

It was an unnerving sequence for me, viewing the film while on sabbatical in Zurich to work on this book. I involuntarily lurched forward in my seat, instinctively protecting my own organs. My body was telling me something that twenty-five years of analysis, study and practice had never put into full focus. I knew at that point what I did not know in the summer of 1964, standing by in my clerical collar supporting student registration of black voters in McComb, Mississippi—only months after the workers' bodies had been found, and only eight years before my arrival in Zurich to begin training as an analyst. Castration anxiety surged through my body and soul.

It might be said that male ferocity is a factor of patriarchal and hierarchical one-upmanship, and is not indigenous to male behavior in general. Yet even in "new age" men one hears constant criticism, even ridicule, of men not liked, disagreed with or perceived as "coming up short." For one man destructively to point out another's shortcomings has a castrating effect, as the word implies. Within the parameters of masculine consciousness, the implicit threat of castration is unavoidable. Phallos is central to masculine identity and power; to diminish another's phallic ownership, size or virility is effectively to diminish the man.

A word here about a related phenomenon, humiliation. James Wyly, in *The Phallic Quest: Priapus and Masculine Inflation*, investigates the necessity of humiliation when a man's phallic stance is inflated. Priapus, a Roman god whose erection was enormous and impossible to relax, a laughing-stock, really, has given his name both to the physical condition of priapism and the related psychological attitude. In such a state, it becomes necessary for a man to be "cut down to size," a process experienced by the man as severely and painfully humiliating. In such a case, humiliation is a remedy, and a necessary one.

Men take pleasure in humiliating one another, whether for cure or for domination, as in the political castrations noted above. It may have been that both Carter and Dukakis were in some way priapic in their attitudes, which made the onslaughts by Reagan and Bush effective, a mixture of cure and domination.

Female-Male Castration

As I was writing this chapter, a news item appeared in the Scranton *Tribune* telling of the arrest of a thirty-one-year-old mother in Everman, Texas. Her five-year-old son had died of alcohol poisoning after he was given more than ten ounces (5/8 pint) of bourbon and told to "drink it like a man." The drink and command were allegedly administered by a male friend of the mother; the mother is accused of negligence.

The interlocking themes of manliness, heroic deed, obedience and death come together in this infuriating story in which castration, taken to its zenith, is an underlying motif. The man friend was charged with first degree felony; the mother's fault was injury to the child by omission. The child's age is classically oedipal. The name of the town should not be overlooked.

"Drink it like a man" is a prototypical castration threat, the father surrogate effectively eliminating his young male competition. He says "be a man" and proceeds to administer the poison his conception of manhood requires. Is the mother unconsciously colluding with her mate against her son? Withal, her standing by is gross and lethal negligence, and castration is seen in stark relief as a deathly consequence. This story vividly illustrates the necessity of taking seriously Freud's insistence upon the reality of childhood sexuality and its continuing influence in the unconscious machinations of adults. The child cannot help but want to be a "man"; the triangle of man, woman, and boy-child as incipient competitor with the man, is again replaed. It demonstrates a transition point between male-male castration and female-male castration. Here the mother stands behind the man's hostility to the boy, passively implicated.

In other situations, the mother takes a clearly active role, maneuvering her son to her advantage. One mother told her young son, growing distant from her as he pressed toward adolescence, "You are killing me," "You used to be such a good boy," "How did the pure gold get changed into vile lead?" "What did I do wrong?" "You don't have your father's energy," and so on. These are recollections of the son some forty years later. Even now, this man experiences himself as something of a dual personality, giving himself two names by which he identifies diametrically different aspects of himself: one sweet and poetic, spiritual, consistent with his mother's expectations, the other out-for-bear, ruthless in professional competition, intellectually concise. Between the two lies a chasm filled with feelings of deep darkness, stress, indecision, intense personal unworthiness—all quite explicable reactions to a continuing threat of castration.

This mother's remarks, echoing the words of the father who urinated in the snow, left a permanent imprint upon the boy. The man carries it still. His mother's price for her love indelibly etched itself into his unconscious and remains there, undercutting the formation of his masculine grid, weakening joints, creating the basis for incomplete masculine transformations. Over and again in analysis, men tell new versions of the old mother-story. The laments now come from lovers and wives. They resonate with the same castrating effect in a man's unconscious. Men flee from them, as from a plague. Or they confront their women with rage. The reprise of the mother's demand is more than they can tolerate.

I find that women often are so unaware of masculine psychology that the vulnerability of men never occurs to them. To an extent, such blindness is understandable, given the excesses of patriarchal domination. Moreover, many women, including feminists who unwittingly accept patriarchal claims of invincibility, see no masculine precariousness. The personal, authentic, nonpatriarchal pain that men express in psychotherapy, however, belies that facile standpoint. Men are fallible human beings, driven by their phallic press for accomplishment, terrified of losing virility, dodging this way and that to protect an inner image of erectile strength. The resistance of women to understanding their men in this way may itself be a factor of an unconscious impulse to castrate, based upon a false image of masculine perfection. Castration is "doubled" in force when a man is not seen as a person in need and then is criticized because he is wounded.

A mother unsure of herself, unconnected to her inherent feminine authority and dignity, can feel compelled to keep her son to herself, emotionally dependent, to maximize her own importance. The mother who has little life of her own trades upon the life she has produced, feeds off it, gradually destroying freedom. Further, a woman who feels dependent upon a man for her very existence cannot freely love such a man; an inner resentment grows, joins with the archetype of the negative or devouring mother, and sets in motion an unconscious process aimed at devastating her captor. When independence falters, neurotic compensation takes place, striking out against the person held responsible for one's imprisonment. Men mindlessly play into this rondelet. They may do it to themselves, reproducing the mother-son arrangement in adult situations. Or they can enforce and reenforce subjection upon a woman, setting the stage for a counterattack.

A particularly grisly depiction of female-male castration can be found in the 1988 Danish film *Pelle, the Conqueror,* set in the nineteenth century. The owner of a Danish farm hires a Swedish immigrant and his young son, Pelle, to do the most menial work, replete with degradation at every turn. Only the owner's wife is more humiliated. She is submitted to the indignity of her husband's drunken trysts with peasants and townsfolk and finally his seduction of her niece, who visits the manor for an extended stay. As the young woman departs, to be accompanied to the station by the owner, the wife, unbeknown to him, discovers that her niece is pregnant, the final straw. On his return, she draws the knife in their bed. Thereafter, her errant husband lies upon a couch, a neutered tomcat, surfeiting himself with bon-bons, sweetly smiling. His wife has him in her power.

As I was putting the finishing touches on this section, Margaret Thatcher resigned as prime minister of Great Britain. Her imperious, diminishing ways appear to have contributed to her downfall. The

New York Times reports that "her manner often sorely tried her own party allies over the years. 'Will you make up your mind' [she is reported to have once asked her Defence Secretary], 'or will Clive [her aide] and I have to make it up for you?' "[55]

Auto-Castration

Men and boys, strange as it may seem, may castrate themselves.[56] Why would a male do such a thing?

The emphasis in this section will be on misplaced, overextended obedience to a parent. A classic illustration of auto-castration under the power of filial compliance is the story of the Phrygian Attis and Cybele, who, like the Babylonian Tammuz and Ishtar and the Phoenician Adonis and Astarte, are a preeminent couple in early mythology. Cybele, the goddess of caverns, personified the earth in its primitive and savage state, exercising dominion over wild beasts.[57] Queen Cybele fell in love with Attis and made him her priest, imposing chastity upon him, typically the son-lover syndrome. Attis, understandably, was restless in his role, fell in love with a woman and broke his vow. Cybele struck him with madness—clearly a punishment for his striking out on his own—and during this madness he castrated himself as an acknowledgment of his guilt.

When Attis recovered his sanity, he discovered what he had done and was about to kill himself in remorse over his self-violation. Cybele turned him into a fir tree, presumably to protect him from a final abnegation. Attis' story became the source of a Phrygian ritual composed of mourning, with a sacred (phallic) fir-tree carried in procession, a feverish dance, bloody mutilations, a commemoration of resurrection, and, finally, rest—quite obviously an expression of

---

[55] Nov. 23, 1990, p. A-13.
[56] The term auto-castration is unfortunately mechanical in tone, but I use it here because of a possible confusion that might result, for Jungians, if the term self-castration were used.
[57] See *New Larousse Encyclopedia of Mythology*, p. 150.

the mysterious quality of male sexuality, castration included. Jung, in a field adjacent to his beloved Bollingen tower, engraved a phallic milestone from a nearby road with the inscription in Greek, "To the most beautiful Attis."[58]

A present-day son who remains, beyond childhood, obedient to his mother effectually castrates himself. His sexual life belongs not to himself but to her. When he does try to live his own life, he feels cursed by a curse similar to Cybele's. If he renews his fidelity, he castrates himself. He becomes Attis. From the standpoint of parental authority, the principals in the story could be king and son as well as queen and son. The sexual motif might be lessened, but the obedience issue, and castration, remain. A son who is afraid to strike out on his own because it might not be in line with the parents' intentions, or might lie outside the family's social conditioning, cuts off his own prowess. This is the "who do you think you are?" syndrome, the byword of a constricted family.

The young hero in the recent film *Dead Poets' Society* was the son of a driving professional father and a docile mother. Inspired by a brilliant teacher at his boarding school—a man who taught and believed Walt Whitman's words that "the powerful play goes on and you may contribute a verse"—the young man followed his love of theater. He played Puck in *A Midsummer Night's Dream.* His father came to the play, dragged the boy home, forbade the bliss. The young man shot himself that night.

A male's guilt in owning his personal/phallic identity can take the form of self-destruction. Once a pattern has been set, to step outside of imposed authority instills guilt. A rearrangement of hierarchies does not happen without disobedience, which in turn gives rise to the possibility of interior authority, and, simultaneously, guilt. Guilt, because it is antagonistic to one's good sense of self, expresses itself in rage. Rage, then, becomes a necessary access point for the challenging of imposed authority. Rage, taken out on oneself, is auto-castration.

---

[58] See above, p. 8, and Aniela Jaffé, *C.G. Jung: Word and Image,* p. 197.

Stepping out of line, typically a boyish attribute, is commonly the way developing phallos is expressed. As the years proceed and the boy becomes a teen-ager and then a man, the introjected inner voice of parental approval/disapproval becomes the fulcrum upon which the issue of castration continues to depend. This is especially crucial in the early years of sexual experimentation. The frightened/obedient teen-ager who will not risk parental disfavor shows the signs of earlier castration injury and, as well, inhibits the restoration of phallos by a newly discovered masculine pride in himself.

When a young man acts sexually, he does so inevitably as one who breaks a law, psychologically. Parental authority establishes an implicit prohibition: the youngster is to stay within the family. Teen-aged sexual activity signals the end of childhood, a movement away from kinship obedience. The stronger the unresolved identity issue is with the mother, the more difficult a natural, sexual moving-out will be for the son.

In one case with which I am familiar, an adolescent son backed away from consummating his first genuine love relationship, in spite of the girl's willingness, due to a fear that doing so would "destroy" his family of origin. Even tentatively to enter the girl would diminish his bond with his mother, the core parent of the family. The irrationality of his fear points to the awesome power of guilt and its connection with auto-castration in the unconscious. Young phallos was depotentiated, with a subsequent adverse effect upon this man's ability to make adult decisions apparently unrelated to sexuality.

A word on Jesus' remark that "there be eunuchs, which have made themselves eunuchs for the kingdom of heaven's sake." [59] Presumably Jesus was speaking about celibacy, lived purposefully as an aid to both ministry and personal salvation. A eunuch is a castrate, and making oneself a eunuch is auto-castration.

Jesus' exhortation is difficult to comprehend. His use of such a graphic, concrete term for self-discipline has led to sexual and erotic mutilations of every sort within the Christian tradition. Because sex-

---

[59] Matt. 19:12, Authorized (King James) Version.

uality and imagination are so closely intertwined, the loss of masculine prowess, particularly when self-inflicted, can be seen as an act of extraordinary devotion. Origen, perhaps the greatest early theologian, castrated himself in an act of literal obedience (presumably) to the injunction, only, it is said, to regret the act later. Jung connects auto-castration to subservience to the Great Mother, as in the Attis myth.[60] Since Origen lived in Alexandria, it may have been that his radical act was reinforced by the proximity and pervasiveness of Great Mother piety.

In contemporary Western life, the closest approximation to making oneself a eunuch for "the kingdom of heaven's sake" is found in the Roman Catholic Church's insistence upon a male and celibate priesthood. Sexuality does not disappear from a man's life with the taking of vows of chastity. Whether a particular priest is sexually active or not, erotic manliness can, and should, be present in his love of his flock, their love of him, in preaching and in ritual celebration.

While a problem is posed as to explicit obedience to church law, there is no way that phallic presence, the outer expression of a man's inner masculine grid, can be suppressed psychologically. The suffering of these man, resulting from an imposed requirement for sexual abstinence in order to live their vocation, is real, but not the result of auto-castration. For priests who force psychological castration upon themselves, enormous problems ensue, including depression, alcoholism, compulsive sexual behavior and the loss of leadership, imagination, vigor and self-esteem. They can, indeed, become unconscious votaries of the devouring aspect of the Great Mother.

Societal Castration

Collective consciousness, often shortened to "the collective," is a term Jungians use to denote dominant cultural patterns, meaning the system of generally accepted values and codes within which everyone is expected to live. The phenomenon is usually understood to be

---

[60] *Symbols of Transformation,* CW 5, par. 392n.

sociological, and therefore not within the purview of a work such as this. But it is also psychological and needs noting, particularly in a Jungian context, where the inner is understood as a reflection of the outer, and the outer of the inner. Today the cultural dominant in the Western world is called patriarchy, the institutionalized diminishment of supposedly inferior persons. Diminishment is cutting-off, and cutting-off in masculine psychology is castration.

Most seriously ostracized today are men of color. In racial stereotyping, black men are seen by whites as more amply endowed genitally. White men are wary. Whether or not the notion is accurate, the size of a man's genitalia computes in the unconscious as a symbol of power, regardless of a particular's man's impact. The influence of the unconscious, and the power of phallos as central symbol in the masculine psyche, is underscored by the persistence of the fantasy. On the rational, collective level, the white man understands himself as cultural "father" to the black. Archetypally, the white man's interior boy unconsciously suspects that he is son to the "larger" black man, the instinctual, better-endowed "father."

Indeed, the white man *is* son if anthropological discoveries finding the origin of humankind in Africa are correct. The white man's fear of the black man continues, as the electoral success of Senator Jesse Helms in North Carolina amply demonstrates. If anthropology coincides with archetype, the white man dominating the "inferior" black is false; the fantasy of black genital superiority finds its compensatory basis in the white man's unconscious and in psychohistory. Black retaliation is not only a faulted effort at survival. It has its origin in the righting of a white-male-ego misconception.

In America, city streets have become captive to young black men, to black male rage, the product of white male social castration. Black men selling drugs, as they do on the streetcorner where I live in New York, black men thieving and attacking pedestrians, can be seen psychologically as desperate personal antidotes to abject defeat. Black young men, for the most part, have no way of entry into white and guarded male precincts of power. What, then, is their recourse? How can they prove their worth? How do they get into competition?

Erich Neumann has described what he calls patriarchal castration.[61] His argument sparks with brilliance, even if based upon a fundamental misconstruction. He discusses the archetype of the Terrible Father, who appears either as the phallic Earth Father or the frightening Spirit Father. The phallic Earth Father castrates through the overwhelming aggressiveness of male sexual instinct, the core fear of whites. The frightening Spirit Father castrates by enforcing the old and established social order, the core despair and rage in blacks. Neumann's schema seems to support the inevitability of castration in masculine development in either mode.

Neumann holds that the Terrible Father, in either guise, is himself the agent of the Great Mother. He contends that the Great Mother encourages physical sexuality and discourages heroic spiritual independence in order to maintain her prominence. The Great Mother holds the hero back through regressive bondage—therefore the danger of physical sexuality to a man, since sexuality is the most flagrant of her enticements. Neumann sees the Great Mother also lurking behind the figure of the frightening Spirit Father prohibiting the son from fending for himself. The son, then, hides behind conventional postures, always afraid of venturing beyond parental confines, as in white patriarchal stereotypic thinking. Neumann substantiates Freud's notion of the superego.

To my mind, Neumann's pervasive error is to consider the masculine—in this case the Terrible Father—as the tool of the Great Mother until a man abandons his physicality and moves into the solar realm of light and spirit.

Patriarchy does indeed castrate males who cannot or will not move into the fraternity of the solar establishment. The black "son," however, may have little choice, so overwhelming are the cards stacked against him. Even if one were to accept Neumann's categories (which I do not), they do not now, and never have, accounted for the man castrated by the system; neither the instinctuality of chthonic Mother nor the collectivity of solar Father are options for him.

---

[61] *The Origins and History of Consciousness,* pp. 186-190.

Neumann's system is not only pervasively patriarchal, it is also unconscionably elitist.

The black man stands awash in hopelessness vis-a-vis the system, with neither primal religion nor capitalist aspiration to assuage his amputation. Antisocial behavior may be the only resort. Either that, or the rest of one's life in a veterans' hospital, never to recover from a war he never asked to fight. Patriarchy will always ask someone else to make the supreme sacrifice.

But the black man is not alone in disaster. The man who has a choice, and does choose to conform, suffers his own kind of societal castration. He may not even know he suffers, a condition that is, in its own way, equally devastating. The outer reward for remaining within the gratifying confines of the Mother, of buying into the power structures of the Father, is substantial. But the man becomes a clone, knowing just the right thing to say at a business meeting or cocktail party, knowing what is *au courant* like the back of his hand, but vacuous in his soul.

Addendum. Men who debauch are smothered in unconscious maternal containment. However, a man who continues to live sexually throughout his life is not thereby and perforce castrated by mother containment, as Neumann suggests. Masculine sexuality is a spiritual as well as a physical enterprise. Neumann's notion that the Great Mother rules all physicality is incorrect. It smacks of Freud, not Jung, *à la* terror of the unconscious. Phallos is physical and phallos is masculine and phallos is spiritual. I know as a male that an essential aspect of sexual rejuvenation is sexuality's regressive character. The deconstructive (ego-relativizing) quality of regression opens the door to encountering a veil of mystery, where one meets and eventually drinks deeply of soul. The point is that regression returns one not only to the mother. That is the purpose in my establishment of phallos as co-equal with the feminine in the primal unconscious.[62]

---

[62] See above, notes 4 and 6.

Castration by Fate

The castration delivered by fate is a "just-so" story. To include fate as an agent of castration goes against our contemporary fixation on causality and personal responsibility—the how-it-happened and how-to-fix-it compulsiveness of modern life. Impotence, actual or symbolic, happens and it may be no one's "fault."

In the summer of 1986 I was en route from the Dordogne section of France to Brussels to board a flight to New York. I was changing trains in Paris, my arms full of luggage and packages. Shortly before the departure of the train, I realized I would arrive late in Brussels and leave early the next morning for New York, and that it would be smart to have both Belgian francs and US dollars. I found the exchange office and inched along in line with my bundles. After the transaction, I slipped my wallet into a side pocket of my jacket. After trundling my belongings to a sandwich stand, I discovered that my wallet was gone—no money, no credit cards, no travelers checks. (Luckily my train and air tickets and passport were in an inside pocket.) It was hard for me to believe, after my inspiration and self-satisfaction at my foresightedness.

The late-evening ride to Brussels was a mixture of panic, dejection and rage at both myself and the unfairness of the world. My ability to "do" had been taken from me by a stranger's hand.

Castration? Not titanic, of course, but surely deflation, helplessness, powerlessness—a micro example of what men experience in a macrocosmic way. Somebody did this to me, but it was an unknown somebody, nobody I could specifically blame. I could rationalize my impotence by arguing that I had been unconsciously but purposely careless, that the thief needed what I had more than I did, that some basic law of equalization had taken place. Yet my sense of loss was not entirely assuaged. I had been violated and spent the hours on the train emotionally bleeding, wondering how I would survive.[63]

---

[63] How I did survive will be told in the next chapter, as an example of one possible antidote to castration.

Sometimes things just happen and we cannot sort them out. Or it is beyond our ken, in the sense that anyone's ken, or any philosophy's ken, has a limit of effective analysis. Fateful castrations occur to males and, from the perspective of fate, they are not attributable to male or female opposition, to some clouded personal intention to do oneself in, or to faulty systems. I know of a boy who was born without a functioning anus. Now eight, he suffers the indignity of being radically different from his peers, a situation which will surely affect the strength of his phallic security as he grows older. All bodies are not created equal, a fact that affects not in the least a male's subjective experience of castration anxiety relative to the inequality.

Our modern shyness concerning fate is a rational resistance to explaining the inexplicable by referring to the will of God. Rationality, however, as Jung well knew, is a function of the will, and it is precisely that which is impervious to will power that is most puzzling to the ego. Depth psychology often participates in a rationalistic cause-and-effect fantasy in spite of its commitment to the concept of the unconscious. If one knows the cause, one can dispel the problem. Fateful castration contradicts and eludes rationalistic solution. "In practice", wrote Jung, "chance reigns everywhere . . . . The plenitude of life is governed by law and yet not governed by law, rational and yet irrational."[64] That which is not governed by law might be governed by purpose, as Jung often suggested. Yet there are insults to phallic stamina that seem even beyond the scope of purpose. They seem quite meaningless and arbitrary, unyielding to moralizing.

A visitation of inhibiting chance on one's phallic satisfaction and maturity could well cause a groundswell of rage in a man against the excruciating unfairness of fate, a hand that has been dealt with little or no possibility of success. In the spectacular Swedish documentary, *The Miracle of Life*, one watches in amazement the struggle of sperm to survive the rigors of ejaculation within the body of a woman, millions falling by the wayside. The viewer is reminded by the commentator that the one victorious sperm able to inseminate the

---

[64] *Two Essays on Analytical Psychology,* CW 7, par. 72.

ovum might well be defective in chromosomes, producing a flawed conception. Jung's words about life "not governed by law" reverberate in one's mind and give pause to any kind of easy conclusion as to design. One is given rationality as a human gift, an evolutionary accomplishment, an opportunity for understanding and growth. But rational understanding is limited. At the entry of chance, reason can do little but move aside. Ego control—will power—has little to do with the survival of sperm in the vagina, to say nothing of the constitution of the successful seed and egg.

Castration anxiety, male angst over the annihilation of the masculine, is as deeply rooted within the masculine psyche as the fate of sperm in ejaculation. One gets a sense of the archetypal basis of the masculine storming of the castle, wave after wave mowed down, throughout history. The egg sits as Penelope awaiting Odysseus, as Psyche awaiting Eros, as the Irish wives in the plays of Synge awaiting return of their lost sea captains. The crucial difference between the masculine and the feminine is clarified.

Natural wisdom tells a male that catastrophic consequence is always present, actually or potentially, as in the fate of his sperm. In the language of this work, such catastrophic consequence is imaged as castration. Here, the need for Jung's religious view of psyche becomes apparent. Fate, or chance, leaves open a space within which an intuitive basis for anxiety is both respected and valued. What the sperm experiences in its life struggle toward ovum is the ground or archetypal pattern for a man's daily struggle for virility. Body awareness that but one sperm will succeed, two million will die, is the raw material of masculine psyche, the fuel for a male's terror of fate. Not only does a man's erection die, and with it his precious erotic urge. So also do two million potential replicas of himself.

In Greek mythology the three Fates are feminine spirits; in Scandinavian mythology the three Norns are also feminine. The Fates have been defined as "the individual and inescapable destiny which followed every mortal being."[65] Given the struggle of sper-

---

[65] *New Larousse Encyclopedia of Mythology,* p. 163.

matazoa, this is not surprising. Nature's wisdom is translated into story; chance, having no relationship to personal worth, is personified as feminine, the containing vessel—the battlefield—of masculine survival. Among the Fates, Clotho is the spinner of the thread of life, Lachesis is the element of luck, Atropos is inescapability. All three Norns are spinners.

Chance can give to a man no issue at all. Chance can give him a brilliant child; as well, it can give a deformed child, needing intensive care the rest of its life. Chance also gives quite ordinary children, products of quite ordinary sperm. Love, at its best, does not judge the value of children because they are ordinary or exceptional, or even one's own. But, ah, love, itself a mystery, is of the feminine. It bends the form of masculine intentionality.

Ontological Castration

A man can experience an entire rejection of what he knows as the foundation for his life. His sense of his own being becomes fragile, inducing in him an unbearable sense of deprivation. He has the inner perception that he is losing his grip on his own existence, that his substance is invisible, unheard, unbelieved. There seems to be no confirmation of his ground, I would say of his metaphoric phallic base. He may know himself, but lacking affirmation from others, his self-confidence is shattered. Because men are so closely tied to an inner need for outer, and effectual, phallic presence, such a situation produces a subjective condition that in severe instances approximates an experience of nonbeing, verging upon annihilation.

The Swiss psychiatrist Ludwig Binswanger founded *Daseinsanalyse,* an existentialist school of psychoanalysis, as an alternative to Freud and Jung. Following Martin Heidegger, Binswanger held the universal human experience of isolation and the menace of nonbeing to be the source of human anxiety and mental illness.[66]

---

[66] See Medard Boss, *Psychoanalysis and Daseinanalysis.* Boss, also a Swiss psychiatrist, further evolved this approach of Daseinanalysis, drawing from

Castration and Male Rage 97

I had an analysand who called his own anxiety a "phallic depth wounding." He applied twice to Jung institutes for training and in both instances was turned down without, he felt, a serious recognition of his worth or the validity of his inner knowledge. His experience may have been the result of a personal trauma and narcissistic wounding that was not overcome, of his father complex standing in his way, etc., etc. Yet, as I listened to him, I was not altogether sure that I myself saw his whole truth. I heard a resonance, a genuine interior grasp of feeling that clearly connected with Jung's discoveries. I began to distrust my own proclivity to psychoanalytic reduction. This man taught me another way to understand castration.

It may be that this man is not meant to be an analyst, that his talent, self-knowledge and familiarity with symbol belong elsewhere, no matter how highly he values acceptance into what he considers to be an elite group. *Macht nichts;* the subjective experience of castration remains. Regardless of what this man should do about himself, he feels rejected, thrown to the dogs, ontologically devastated. It feels as though phallos will never renew, that the tides have run out, that indeed castration and nonbeing are psychologically similar.

One is reminded of Jung's description of the aftermath of his break with Freud, when he experienced "a period of inner uncertainty . . . . a state of disorientation."[67]

> I suspected there was some psychic disturbance in myself. . . . It was a painfully humiliating experience to realize that there was nothing to be done except play childish games. . . . I began accumulating suitable stones, gathering them partly from the lake shore and partly from the water. And I started building . . . a castle.[68]

On my sabbatical in Zurich during the writing of this work, I visited both Jung's home in Küsnacht, where the "childish games" took

---

both Heidegger and Binswanger. The German *da-sein,* usually translated as "existence/existential," is meant to have the connotation "being-there," as in a literal translation (*da*=there, *sein*=being/to be). The focus of Daseinanalysis is the totality of a person's being.
[67] *Memories, Dreams, Reflections,* p. 170.
[68] Ibid., pp. 173-174.

place, and the castle-retreat he subsequently built and embellished along the lake at Bollingen. I saw, in Küsnacht, the substantial remains of one of his "childish" castles on the shore, still embedded with the colored stones he collected. And then the fortress at Bollingen. I realized, as never before, the enormous power essential rejection has for a man, and the extraordinary simplicity required to trust again in the validity of oneself and one's substance.

Rage

It appears to me that beneath the surface of rage lurks anger that has for some time lain unexpressed and surely unrecognized. Beneath anger lies hurt, stemming from an injury causing serious pain.

Stephen Martin has pointed out that rage is "an instinctive reaction which happens automatically and unconsciously, typically in response to some perceived threat," whereas anger is "a conscious feeling state which has about it a sense of judgment, choice, and differentiation."[69]

Martin's distinction suggests that anger is a developed form of rage, consciously recognized and therefore more containable. This makes sense on a structural basis. On a temporal basis, however, it seems to me that pain comes first, then an inner revulsion with the experience of a hurt that is self-denying. When the stakes are raised, rage erupts as a rejection of the unbearable.

Martin does put his finger on rage as an instinctive response to (presumably) an instinctual threat, which is germane to my connecting rage to castration in masculine psychology. Of course I do not claim that castration anxiety is the sole cause of male rage. I do, however, understand there to be a relationship between the two. Confronted by male rage, one must look beneath the rage to the anger, and beyond the anger to the injury causing the pain.

The eruption of male rage signals the presence of instinctual danger—archetypal danger, in Jungian language—and with it, a sense of

---

[69] "Anger As Inner Transformation," p. 32.

desperation. Or, worse, a sense that catastrophe has already taken place, that the man is therefore powerless, without phallos—castrated. If Freud's establishment of infantile sexuality is fundamentally accurate, self-preservation for a male is inextricably related to phallos. The tornado of emotional response in rage has its source in the urgency a man feels to protect and salvage his identity, his very being—that, and/or retaliation for the offence laid upon him, as this is subjectively perceived. Anger may be the emotion one feels when something can be done. Rage is more likely to result when a man feels powerless.

Whether or not a man "should" feel so strongly about himself is not the issue here. Rage is an arc of emotion which by-passes intermediate and more rational anger, drawing its archetypal power from the depth of the masculine instinctual life force. Rage is a last resort. Often its force is proportionate to the intensity of anger that has been repressed. Rage is impacted, stored up, "pressure-cooked" primal anger.

Once a survival threshold level of threat to phallos is perceived by a male—wherever that threshold may be for a given man—the rage response, according to Martin, is automatic. Martin is interested in the transformation of rage into anger, the process by which Aphrodite, goddess of love, opens the souls of men—which he sees enacted in the dramatic encounter between Ares and Hephaestus, the first her lover, the second her betrayed husband. Something of this sort can take place in a man when he reaches the stage of individuation, where the integration of his feminine side becomes a psychological requirement and no longer instigates phallic threat.

One must be careful, however, not to by-pass or civilize rage before its intrinsic connection to castration is understood. Misshapen Hephaestus, Aphrodite's cuckolded husband, discovers his wife and handsome Ares in bed together. In a rage, albeit quiet and crafty, Hephaestus literally "lowers the boom" upon them, a net he devised by his metalworking craftiness. Hephaestus' net is an outer form of his own intact masculine grid and the grid appears in justifiable protection (and projection) of his phallic nature. Furthermore, Hephaestus' lameness, a critical aspect of his characterization, may well point to his phallic vulnerability, since the leg, especially the thigh, has long been understood to have a symbolic phallic significance.[70] The scene has its comic side; the watching Olympians howl with laughter. A friend has said that he has always imagined Aphrodite looking up from under and responding to the mirth of the gods with a petulant, "It's *not* funny!"

Expressions of rage on the part of men threatened by castration is both natural and inevitable, however disconcerting. Rage is an almost inevitable response to omnipresent castration anxiety, and it may be a necessary one if castration is not simply to be endured. Endurance in this context is not transformation. It is passive resignation, a state in which Freud's connection of castration and passivity in men makes sense. Hephaestus could not be considered a god were he to sit by while his extraordinary wife consorted with a competitor. The gods' enjoyment of Hephaestus' capturing of the illicit lovers revived his limpid phallos. Rage, wiliness, humor and restoration belong together.

And then there is Odysseus' rage at the insult poured upon him under his own roof. He returns to Ithaca after ten years' absence following the conquering of Troy, after wandering among seas and islands, encountering every manner of heroic challenge. Disguised as a beggar, Odysseus discovers full force the corruption laid upon his island by the Suitors, princes of nearby places who took advantage of his absence to vie for the hand of Penelope, his wife and queen. Since Odysseus had been so long gone, both Penelope and the Suitors assumed he would not return. The time was approaching when she must choose a new husband from among them.

Odysseus begs money from the Suitors, who laugh at him and deride him. Antinous, a Suitor leader, flings his footstool at him. "Silent [Odysseus] shook his head, brooding on evil."[71] Odysseus is further abused by the regular palace beggar, Irus ("Get up, old man,

---

[70] See R.B. Onians, *The Origins of European Thought*, pp. 182-183.
[71] George Herbert Palmer, trans., *The Odyssey of Homer*, p. 277.

and leave the door-way, or you will soon be dragged off by the leg.")[72] and Melantho, a palace maiden ("Why, silly stranger, you are certainly some crack-brained person . . . you prate continually. . . . Surely the wine has touched your wits; or else it is your constant way to chatter idly.")[73] Odysseus is calm on the surface, but his "brooding on evil" leads to his slaughtering the Suitors.

Odysseus muscles his rage until the finale. The mockery, the vile, inferior men who presumed upon his absence, their pretentiousness at claiming his wife and his kingdom, are classic, a reason why George Palmer claims that the Odyssey "has probably affected western civilization more deeply than any piece of writing outside the Bible."[74] But is Odysseus' outrage a product of what I have been claiming in this work to be the threat of castration?

Yes, if one understands that castration is equivalent to the diminishment of masculine identity and honor. Once the Suitors were eliminated and Odysseus and Penelope were reunited,

> they came gladly to their old bed's rites . . . . [And] when the pair had joyed in happy love, they joyed in talking too, each one relating: she . . . what she endured at home . . . ; he . . . what miseries he brought on other men.[75]

Phallic accomplishment was implicit in the ordeals of Odysseus' journey and it was his goal in returning to Ithaca and his sufferance of insult.

All recipients of rage are victims, whether or not there has been provocation. When the tables are turned, there can be humor. But there is nothing humorous about the enormous loss others experience as a result of emotional and physical abuse by rageful men. Nothing can justify the mayhem often left in its wake, including child abuse, wife beating, murder. My point here is simply to fathom the connection between rage and castration rather than to moralize about it or

---

[72] Ibid., p. 282.
[73] Ibid., p. 292.
[74] Ibid., p. xi.
[75] Ibid., p. 367.

prescribe its cure.

Male rage is an indication that a man is in living and excruciating personal contact with profound injury, even nonbeing. One can receive or observe such rage and shrink from it, judging it with appropriate harshness, but without a modicum of understanding. Women do so, unaware that they are implicated in the damage against which the rage is drawn. Men do so, secure in their victory over a vanquished phallic competitor. Children, of course, cannot be expected to understand, for they are innocent of the trials faced by the hero who will never be a hero, the hopeless effort of a father to be what he is not and cannot be.

I hear, again and again, tales from their sons of drunken Pennsylvania coal-mining/railroading/factory fathers who returned home after the saloon ranting at life, at unsatisfied wives and demanding children, at the rich owners, at their crummy rented shack houses with furniture torn at the seams, at a government that gave them little for their taxes. I have a measure of sympathy for those fathers and their despair. Their sons suffered greatly at their hands. The fathers suffered greatly at the hands of life.

I have a respect for male rage, a respect which comes from my respect for phallos and a knowledge of the inner terror instigated by the intimation of its loss. The desperation a man feels when his sense of self is ripped away, trampled upon, belittled, ignored, is horrendous.

I recall an unforgettable moment with my father. He was lying in bed, having returned home after a year in a veterans' hospital where he was treated for tuberculosis, which turned out to be emphysema. The illness signaled the end of his career, even his life. Perhaps I was twenty years old at the time. Something came up about his illness and I offered the facile opinion that he was not having enough fun in life, that he ought to look at my friend Jim and what a carefree person he was. My father reached across the bed and slapped me squarely in the face. I had never before experienced my father's desperation. I knew nothing, then, of his pain, his inner sense of defeat. Now, when I am sixty, I am learning.

All feeling and emotion that men experience is not attributable to the anima, their feminine side. And all advice to men that they should express their emotions, "let it out," is not good advice. The integration of the feminine is another matter altogether. This became clear to me in an incident years ago during a month-long stint at Esalen, the human-potential center in California.

Some thirty theologically oriented people were sponsored by a foundation that was curious to know if religious professionals might find something of value in humanistic psychology. At one point I became the focus of an encounter group, sitting in the center. A woman who did not like me very much began a verbal barrage, standing over me, pouring out abuse. I sweltered. The leader told me to respond in kind. I refused. Had I done so, I might have broken the limits of decent human behavior. The killer instinct was rising in me.

Just so, men often keep their emotions under cover because they are frighteningly strong. Yet the situation can be quite different from my Esalen experience. A couple once came to me for counseling because the man refused to talk. The woman was driven to distraction; his behavior produced every kind of negative projection in her. A tide turned in their relationship after I suggested, in a private session with him, that the woman was "thick skinned," that she was strong and fair and probably could take what he had to say.

In fact, the man had nothing very terrible to say, but he had been accustomed to women berating and dominating him. He would shut up and steam. He claimed that he did not want to hurt his friend and by so saying admitted that he was afraid of what he might say and do. Once he began to talk, he discovered that he could tell this particular woman what he was thinking and how he felt, without her taking advantage of his insecurities and causing the return of his dreaded rage. He had been mistaken on two counts. He had misread his woman and misread himself.

Phallic power, pleasure and pain constitute the biological basis of masculine psychological life. Unless one understands this, male rage is incomprehensible. To ignore a man, to diminish him, to remove his sense of potency, prestige and purpose compels him, after the phallic paradigm, to rise in defense of himself, however misguided, futile or dangerous that defense might be.

Rage is pseudo-phallos, a faulted effort to express manliness, to lash out against its perceived injury or removal. It don't make it right, but it happens.

The Paradox of Castration

That which a male wants most to avoid he must encounter for his masculinity to be established and to evolve. Men protect phallos with every means at their disposal. Yet castration cannot be avoided.

Thus the castration element in masculine psychology is paradoxical. A man must go through castration, neither evading it nor remaining within its pall of injury. Castration is a threat to a man in each developmental stage—his phallic substance either increases, both in outer importance and inner significance, or it stalemates, experienced as emasculation.

One is reminded of the paradoxical Jewish and Christian injunctions: "To every thing there is a season . . . . A time to get, and a time to lose; A time to keep, and a time to cast away";[76] and "He that findeth his life shall lose it: and he that loseth his life . . . shall find it."[77] There is no way to be firmly connected with phallos without the element of castration within the process; conversely, there is no engagement in the rigors of castration without the promise of phallos as a renewable reward. Were this not so, no male would undergo the trials of masculine transformation.

When a man evades the ordeal, he forever suspects that he has embarked on a course of failure. The suspicion nags him, and often the suspicion is valid. Male oversensitivity often circles around this issue. As he traverses the masculine transformations of younger years, a male cannot know the consequences of his life transitions or the small, seemingly forgettable moments when crucial paths are taken. Yet something within him "knows," and as the years pass this

---

[76] Eccles. 3:1,6, Authorized (King James) Version.
[77] Matt. 10:39, Authorized (King James) Version.

knowledge gnaws at him. It can return in dream images or life situations, long afterward, that reprise the old circumstance, sometimes literally, sometimes obliquely.

A man tells me that his mother would take him as a boy to visit relatives in a formal tea-party setting, expecting him to behave as a little gentleman, sitting straight in a chair, while the adults made conversation. The boy hated these visits and everything within him struggled for and against staying in that chair. Usually he was obedient, afraid to disobey. Forty years later, his wife expects him at the dinner table when she is finished cooking; he is on the telephone in another part of the house to a friend in need. When he enters the kitchen, his wife is angry and he is momentarily frozen in fear.

The paradox involves taking risk, fearing that one will be hurt, rejected or judged, but risking nonetheless, knowing that otherwise one is disloyal to oneself. The hurt for a male is the prototype of castration; the loyalty to one's own needs, one's inner truth, is the prototype of phallic necessity. The fact that every man (unless he's crazy) is afraid of some aspects of women, bosses, risks, points up the inevitability and omnipresence of castration threat to men. But males who habitually hold back, letting fear rule, become afraid of anything that suggests potential castration. They find themselves afraid of all women, superiors, of any situation or confrontation where they might lose.

The power of women to threaten masculine security is an established experience for a dispositionally frightened man. His answer is sabotage, distance, domination, the social implements of patriarchy. The power of men to threaten a man's self-confidence is underwritten by the archetype of father-castration. A fearful response is retreat, a kind of cringing, proceeding from a lack of inner knowledge that phallos returns, that it has an intrinsic and natural capacity for self-restoration. Such knowledge can be gained only by the experience of loss and the discovery of subsequent renewal, the disappearance and reappearance of phallos, building a trust in the presence and strength of one's masculine grid.

In a discussion of psychological problems encountered in the tran-

106 Castration and Male Rage

sition from the first half of life to the second, Jung commented that "a dissociation is not healed by being split off but by a more complete disintegration"—the psychic principle of paradox, which applies to castration. Jung continued (and here I ask the reader to keep the castration issue in mind):

> All the powers that strive for unity, all healthy desire for selfhood, will resist the disintegration, and in this way he will become conscious of the possibility of an inner integration, which before he had always sought outside himself. He will then find his reward in an undivided self.[78]

One learns in Jungian analysis that dreams of dismemberment, which occur often to both males and females, may be portents of rebirth. The alchemical stages called *separatio, divisio, putrefactio, mortificatio* and *solutio* state the necessity of taking apart what the ego understands as unity in order to begin a process that not only restores, but moves beyond restoration toward a new creation. How it can be that the most treasured personal feature of masculinity, the characteristic of a male that puts its stamp upon the attributes of his gender, must be lost before it is truly possessed is a mystery embedded within the enigma of paradox. In the defeat of phallos (disintegration, in Jung's description) lies, strangely, the essence of its victory. Men know this in the exhaustion which follows ejaculation, necessarily preceding subsequent erection.

Another mythological parallel to the paradox of castration can be seen in the Hindu story of Kali, often depicted as a fierce, hideous, devouring goddess, one of the many forms of the wife of Shiva. A portrayal of the negative mother par excellence, Kali is shown adorned with hacked-off heads and hands, drinking the blood of her victims and consuming their entrails.[79] The dire threat of castration is extended, in Kali, to the entire body, to life itself.

---

[78] "Marriage As a Psychological Relationship," *The Development of Personality*, CW 17, par. 334.

[79] See Erich Neumann, *The Great Mother*, pp. 147-149, and *New Larousse Encyclopedia of Mythology*, p. 335.

And yet, as Jung said, "History teaches us over and over again that, contrary to rational expectation, irrational factors play the largest, indeed the decisive, role in all processes of psychic transformation."[80] Kali, herself, serves a positive psychological purpose, in and through the primordial darkness of her destruction. Thus David Kinsley in *The Sword and the Flute* calls attention to her benign aspect. By moving into her apocalyptic vortex, a man overcomes the opposites of good and evil, appearances and essence, hope and despair, life and death. The assimilation of "Kali-reality" transforms her into a vehicle of salvation, and her victim's sacrifice into a victory over maya, the veil of illusion. Even as she herself is a portrayal of gross matter, Kali points the way to relief from imprisonment in the endless cycle of pain and sorrow that is experienced in life.

Caught, enmeshed in the midst of the process, a man rages at his fate. He can see neither beginning nor end in his moment of siege. What a man must trust, what he can know if he pays attention to phallos, is that heading into diminishment is the way out of diminishment. Phallos performs, dies, returns to life. Castration is the death. Resurrection is predicated on the next day's erection.

In the Egyptian myth of Osiris, the great king, and Isis, his queen, Osiris' body is torn asunder by Set, his jealous brother. Set scatters the pieces of Osiris' body all over the place. His penis lands in the sea. Isis has the job of collecting the pieces in order to reconstitute Osiris' regality and paternity, but the penis is lost. Isis, despairing over her husband's castration, fashions a new penis and appends it to Osiris, restoring his virility. Wonderously, Joseph Campbell suggests: "The missing piece, the genital organ, has been swallowed by a fish. This is the origin of the fish meal on Fridays; it's a sacramental consuming of the sacred flesh."[81] Which suggests that while Catholics were eating fish on Friday, they were unknowingly consuming the phallos of the Egyptian god.

Paradox indeed.

---

[80] *Symbols of Transformation,* CW 5, p. xxvii.
[81] *Transformations of Myth Through Time,* p. 83.

4
Coming to Terms with Castration

If a man gets wind of a castration issue within himself, there are a number of—well, not exactly cures—but antidotal actions he might take. Castration is never cured, in the sense that it is eliminated as a masculine problem. But a man need not leave his castration as he finds it.

Nor should he. Every man has the personal responsibility to put himself into the way of restoration, consciously cooperating with the inherent proclivity of phallos to reappear and reform after its own demise. According to Jung, the psyche seeks ways to make itself whole; it is self-regulating, self-healing. This is clearly the case in the capacity phallos has to spring again to life, reenergized and poised, even though battered and bruised by circumstance. Beyond a man's blaming of someone else for his condition, he needs to look at himself and his intrinsic potential for self-healing. A man needs to weep, it is true, and he needs also to take charge of himself.

But I am a bit ahead of myself. A prior question is: how does a man make an inner check to ascertain whether his problem is castration, or, better said, whether it is more of a problem than need be? What questions does he ask in a personal inventory of his situation? What are the signs, the prodromal indications?

Signs of Castration

The first thing for a man to examine is his level of rage. Some men quite easily, all too easily to suit those who live with them, fly off the handle. In a sense, these are the lucky ones, those who are not so carefully guarded and repressed in their emotional lives that they do not even experience their own terror.

Men who suspect that they make problems of themselves need only ask if they are a nuisance. But even if the asking is never done, people tell them so or they get signals of displeasure.

One clear sign is the damage they can see inflicted upon their loved ones, the others' avoidance, a coldness of heart engulfing their living space. Another is the failure of their professional interests; they never get anywhere. Still another is a growing sense of embarrassment, even shame, when a memory of an outbreak returns. Everybody, man and woman alike, is afraid of male rage. It rips open the seams of the garment of life. It is rapacious and intrusive, phallic in a desperate way.

There are men who do not vent their rage but seethe, churning and foaming as if just about to boil over. One gets a sense of meanness, of a petcock about to explode on a pressure cooker, an on-the-verge disappointment and almost-hidden resentment. Someone is always ahead of this man; his wife and children hold him down, or his parents, or his friends, or his boss . . . or . . . or. It might be said that there is so much fear in such men that they dare not express it; what little they have would tumble down.

And there are men who do not even seethe; they are almost too calm, without the energy of seething. They try very hard to be nice, and nice they are, usually, but without the muscle that comes from phallos and gives a masculine tone to manner. One gets the impression that the niceness is not altogether genuine, that it is a cover, that something is lurking within that dare not show its face. In this case, resentment is really hidden, not just almost. It takes living with a person who is impositionally nice to know just how strange such an even goodness is. It affects an unwavering equanimity which makes anyone else's expression of displeasure appear to be vulgar.

Any man, no matter how calculated his personally imposed constraint, has a threshold that cannot tolerate violation. This is the boundary of his castration anxiety, and it can be broached somehow, somewhere, sometime. The old maxim, "Scratch a Turk and get a Tartar" expresses the situation well.

A second sign of castration is overconstruction. This is my term for a kind of defence against anxiety that fills the holes and smooths the surface, laying on that surface a fabrication of activity that obscures the awareness of weakness. The aim is to close any entrance to the unconscious, and so dazzle the eye with a new skyline that the undercurrents of inadequacy will never be noticed. Pseudo-phallos is the presenting image. Overconstruction is a compensation, suggesting an undiscovered, avoided, sense of phallic enfeeblement.

As I write this, a number of overconstructed empires have recently fallen: Michael Milken of Drexel Burnham Lambert in the financial world, Robert Campeau in department stores, Father Bruce Ritter in social services, Donald Trump in everything. In each case, the reach was too high, as though the phallos one had was not enough, that it had to be bigger, greater, more noticeable than anyone else's.[82]

I speak here of the man who obsessively builds, who is heroic to a fault. This man cannot relax his efforts. He must always prove himself, always do something useful, always be hard at it, as though the least softening of effort would reveal a hidden weakness. His mind spins fantasies of new accomplishments even when on the beach or the ski trail. He must have a telephone in his car, in his bathroom. He lays grid upon masculine grid, and grid upon that grid, not burnishing a delicate corner in a fine way, but endlessly manufacturing. He is heavy industry; pastoralia is foreign territory. This is not quite the same thing as being "too big for one's britches," itself a sign of castration compensation. The "too big" man does little in construction, assuming that his views are true because he thinks they are.

I often catch myself in an overconstructionist syndrome. I fly to Tucson from Scranton on Friday to give a presentation, speaking that night and leading a workshop all day Saturday. I spend Sunday flying back to New York. I work analytically on Monday and Tuesday, moving my Wednesday hours forward a day. Then, because I have no car in New York and because I must get copy to my publisher in three days, I take an 11:00 p.m. bus back to Scranton on Tuesday,

---

[82] The overconstruction of the United States shows itself in the Bush-led obsession to force its will upon the Arab World with a superior weaponry that is patriarchally priapic. Intimations of collapse and impending humiliation abound.

arriving at 1:30 a.m., and continue my editing all day Wednesday. Then Thursday, a day of more analytic hours, then Friday an all-day meeting for a conference, then Saturday editing ... then ... then.

A third indication of castration is the opposite of overconstruction: timidity. Timidity is often mistaken for modesty, but there is an important difference. Modesty in a man is the product of his secure and tenured sense that he is honored by his membership in a tribe marked by its phallic identity. The modest man knows from experience that while he may not be as big as the next man, what he has works and counts, and he has no reason to feel inferior, or, in a compensatory way, to think too highly of himself. He is confident in his membership; he has passed muster. It is difficult to understand a man's inner sense of security without an inference of gender adequacy. Our use of language is sexually suggestive; member, etymologically, derives from flesh. Metaphor, like the archetype, has its basis in actual masculine erotic experience. Its source is biological.

Timidity, on the other hand, takes its energy from shame and embarrassment, from an inner sense of not being genuinely phallic, of not being important as a male in the world of men. A timid man suspects that he does not make a difference, that he is actually or psychologically impotent. A timid man is nervous, fearful, skittish. Every man is fearful when it comes to a challenge for which he is not suited; fear is a manly attribute in its appropriate place, as the hero's story tells. What I speak of here is an overarching personality characteristic. A timid man will keep his mouth shut when it should be open. He will hide himself, keep his phallos in his trousers when a situation requires its display.

Instead of expressing with his words what Jung, after the alchemists, called *logos spermatikos*—speech thrust from a mind that acts as a spiritual phallos—the timid man is crippled, limp ... and silent. A timid man will hide in his house, his corporate office, his fishing shack, his labor union, his church, when something tells him he ought to be on a front line, interjecting himself against something he opposes. The timid man is the heel under his wife's slipper, dominated by her needs, her requirements, her running of the ship.

A timid man's woman generally has the authority of phallos, coming from her patriarchal animus. He, on the other hand, shows signs of psychological infirmity.

Rage, overconstruction and timidity are three ways in which one can ascertain the presence of castration. But then what? What can a man do? *Doing* is archetypally phallic in its determination and point, its inherent need to make. *Being* is archetypally feminine in its earthy, loamy richness, its presence and fecundity. Depending upon where a man is in his phallic development, he must do and/or be in a way that furthers his inner transformation. If his masculinity is injured—and only a particular man can know how true this is for himself—the requirement for him is to *do*.

Antidotes to Castration

Mentoring

Mentoring is an animation of the father archetype. The primal father-son connection never leaves a man's life. A son is a smaller version of the father. A father is a larger version of the son. A father wants his son to be like himself, and if the father is a liberated man he wants his son to be a larger version of himself. Larger/smaller are, once again in masculine psychology, phallic comparatives. A son, early on, is aware that his father is large, that he, the son, is small. A son grows into largeness through the emulation of his father if a castration impediment does not intervene. Psychologically stymied men always feel threatened by a larger man. Mythically, the focus quite naturally falls upon phallos and its derivatives.

To what extent can a natural father initiate his son into the world of men? The complexities of oedipal competition, the impediments of castration memory, the incest taboo, hinder the process. A mentor, however, can participate in essential father-son archetypal energies without the implications of castration inherent in the blood relationship. He can further a younger man's need for filial independence, encouraging him without the constraint of a castrating competition for the mother.

One also learns from peers, but transmission of the essence of masculinity comes from an initiated male, one who knows something the novice does not. A natural father is beset in his own entanglement with his son's mother. A mentor is not. Distance, with a consequent symbolization of the father archetype, is the operative factor. A natural father does his son a favor by gracefully releasing his son to discover his masculine heritage for himself.

The ancient Doric tradition of a nobleman transferring his substance to a boy through phallic penetration is one reflection of archetypal mentoring. The practice has fallen away, perhaps due to the potentiality for its abuse: in jumping over the father-incest prohibition, the boy may not have been liberated but further bonded while the mentor was sexually gratified. Without entering into an extended discussion of this issue, let it be said the potency of the father-son archetypal connection and its importance for phallic empowerment is illuminated even in its calumny. Mentoring always depends for its efficacy upon the generosity and clarity of the provider. If the mentor gives with one hand and takes away with the other, archetypal intention is twisted by aggrandizing ego-service.

Peer power grows as mentoring diminishes. As fewer authentic masculine role models and initiations exist, the chaos of peer pressure grows proportionally, so great is the need for a young man to discover masculinity. Male initiation becomes increasingly rare with the loss in society of wise and admirable men who share of themselves. Perverted and destructive behavior can be seen as the product of warped archetypal patterns, left without an effective cultural means for passing on the mystery.

A castrated man needs a seasoned, knowing man as friend and guide. The man need not be chronologically a great deal older. But he must be perceived as more experienced, clearly wise, and friendly. The analyst who did the most to draw me over the line into adult masculinity was ten years my junior. The mentoring relationship, however, need not be explicitly set out as such. A kid can go down to the market and hang around with a storekeeper, climb a tree and watch the man next door in his yard. A young man with little hope can be mentored by a pimp or a dope peddler. What counts is the learner's subjective need for an example of maleness.

Crucial is the mentor's self-possession, conscious or no, as perceived by the other, and his ability and willingness to give what the younger man feels he needs. Learning can be intermittent, as when a younger man, a new father, say, sits with a respected father-in-law long into the night over a bottle of Scotch after dinner, away from the women. Such conversations rarely happen today. The father-in-law may not be interested in the younger man, or may see him as a rival for his daughter's affections, or the young man, fearing rejection—castration—avoids him. The poet Robert Bly, in his lovely work on mentoring, stresses the necessity for older men actively to offer themselves to younger men in the spirit of sharing with others the masculine spirit they themselves contain.[83]

A male can never be certain of another male's friendliness or of immunity from exploitation or attack. Yet the very suspicion one has of the other is an impetus for masculine bonding. Admitting the need for another male—with its undercurrent of the father-son relationship—might seem a diminishment for a man. In a way, of course, it is, exacerbated by the illusion that a real man is never in need of anything. Paradoxically, however, a man's admission of poverty is positive. A different kind of notch in a man's belt may be on the horizon, something not dictated by macho conformity. A mentoring relationship requires humility; an injured man allows another man to point the way.

Touching

In white North American patriarchal society, bodily contact between men is all but forbidden. As men grow older even sporting touch falls away. Hand-shaking alone remains. A man who touches another man for reasons of affection or even by accident is looked upon with suspicion. Male intimacy is taboo. Men are supposed to have themselves too much in hand for that.

---

[83] See Robert Bly and Bill Moyers, *A Gathering of Men.*

Yet physical touching is a fundamental means of giving and receiving personal affirmation. There is no other way for a child to learn about itself or the outer world. And the quality of touch makes a difference. A mother's touch is paramount. A father's touch contributes *his* reality. It has been said that a mother's reality is magnetic, the draw of gravity, while a father's is electric, like a bolt of lightning. A boy needs the touch of his father throughout his growing-up years to grasp his own lightning value, his energy as a male. This need continues throughout life. In point of fact, a version of touching, masturbation, never does end. A man who masturbates is, on some level, reassuring himself as to his possession of phallos.

I once saw a man for another analyst temporarily away from her practice. His need was to recover phallic energy and purpose. I soon became a mentor-figure for him; the connection had strength and vigor. As he left my office one day he surprised me with a long and heartfelt hug. While physical expressions of eros must be carefully monitored in therapy, on this occasion it felt psychologically healing. The man's inner father-need cried out for touch and he had the courage and authenticity to obey it. Another man told me of a talk he had with his father long into the night, accompanied by much drink. As they were going up for the night and the light was turned off, the father gave his son a bear hug; it took liquor and darkness to do it.

Phallos is lightning. It springs from nowhere, jumping and plunging deeply into the earth, striking where it will, without regard to mortal preparedness. Civilization prepares. Phallos, in its naked, chthonic condition, does not. Phallos has its root in instinctuality. Solar phallos is hungry for spiritual power, but spiritual power derives from the rawness of nature, and often masks it.

Georges Bataille writes in *Erotism: Death and Sensuality:*

> Eroticism is an experience that cannot be assessed from outside in the way an object can . . . . Work binds us to an objective awareness of things and reduces sexual exuberance. Only the underworld retains its exuberance.[84]

---

[84] Pp. 149, 155.

116 Antidotes for Castration

An exuberant leap describes precisely the dynamic of my analysand's spontaneous hug, reminiscent of the infant's eager grasping of the father's hand, finger or nose.

Depth psychology understands the underworld, the chthonic, as the repository of instinctual—including sexual—energy. The underworld, the unconscious, is the source from which phallic presence and excitement spring into behavior, as lightning explodes out of darkness. Psychoanalysis is a process of unlocking emotions and feelings hidden behind bulwarks of defense, constructed early on to safeguard a life where touching, among other things, may have gone wrong. The appearance of eros signals a revival of male energy from behind walls of protection.

Male eros carries with it the implication of lightning, sensual arousal. Perhaps touch between males is avoided for this reason. Even as male-female touching has a wondrous effect on phallos, waking it from slumber, so does male-male touching, taboo or not. The body responds to stimulus with its natural wisdom. The excitement of father reconnection prompts the resurrection of maleness. I had an analysand who took baths with his pre-oedipal son. He did not avoid penis touching, natural male play. There were times when both he and the child had erections, laughing at the strange changes taking place. The poverty of restrained and inhibited father-son connection was, for the moment, overcome.

Robert Johnson has defined sensuousness as "the life of the spirit as seen through the senses."[85] Obviously, sensuality is not only sight, but also touch. Johnson's simple definition is wonderful in that it joins spirit and sense whereas conventional wisdom separates and opposes them. More profoundly, Jung knew that each pole of an opposition contains its counterpart—that spirit, indeed, is flesh and that flesh is an expression of spirit, the psychoid aspect of archetype.[86] The fear of touch is the fear of intimacy; intimacy between men suggests masculine vulnerability and thus castration.

---

[85] *Ecstasy, p. 87.*
[86] See above, note 5.

An analysand who was a member of a men's group dreamed:

> I was communicating with various friends (mostly from our men's group) and from the conversations a "close understanding" of each other emerged, a certain naked intimacy. And yet this intimacy did not include any explicit sexual feelings, but was more of a psychic intimacy, even though sexual closeness or appreciation was included in the closeness that was established.

We talked for an hour on the subtle difference between "explicit sexual feelings" and "sexual closeness or appreciation." There was the question of his blocking an awareness, even in the dream, of explicitness as a homosexual taboo, particularly since the words "naked intimacy" were in the dream. It seemed likely to us both that no significant block was present, since he himself raised the question and was aware of rather explicit homoerotic fantasies in waking life. Rather, the dream seemed to point to the connection between deep masculine feeling and its inevitable sensual expression. The depth of sharing between the men in his group activated an awareness of "psychic intimacy," building a "close understanding." The men were growing in trust and appreciation for their shared masculinity, in a way that reflects the picture of the man in his tub with his son. They were all in it together.

From the dream's standpoint, the lack of male intimacy might be seen as a function of male antagonism, expressing the negative element in male relationships, a product of comparison and competition. When men find themselves in cooperation with one another, touch can be a note of reconstruction.

Collegiality

A pervasive medicine for castration is the way men hang out together in clubs, societies, neighborhood bars, sporting associations, labor unions. Intimacy is not an issue in these groups. Rather men gain from each other a sense of common identity, relaxing, pooling their common knowledge and enjoyment in being male. There is neither the distraction of feminine presence nor the competition for favor that always arises when women enter the masculine world.

I remember when I was a young minister in Bemidji, Minnesota. I was single, and alone most of the time. I poured myself into work. A man in the congregation suggested that I join the Lions Club. My first meetings were dreadful—all those noisy and fractious shop owners wolfing down macaroni and cheese, singing ridiculous fraternity songs, collecting money for charity on the basis of gaffes made during the week. Then my friend suggested that I be toastmaster at the annual banquet. I pored over joke books at the public library. The event was a success; mostly, I suspect, because I, as the Episcopal priest, made something of a fool of myself in the use of off-color humor. The point is that after my initiation, I belonged. The men I had judged became my brothers.

Collegiality is based upon belonging to the world of men. A man who hangs at the edge of brotherhood, too busy to join, may be hindered by the fear that he will never belong, cloaked by a vague sense of superiority. Still, something in him wants in. He can stand forever at the window, wondering what connects those inside. He need not be just like the men he joins; chances are he never will be. He may have reservations, as I had with the Lions Club, yet there is a threshold to cross, a common maleness to acknowledge.

Recently I watched a roundtable discussion on National Educational Television about women having a place as front-line infantry personnel. Two men, a general and a congressman, argued against two women, also a general and a member of Congress. The men were outclassed. The women pressed the issue of "what a person can do, a person can do," with no one excluded because of gender. The men's arguments made no logical sense when confronted by the women's superbly honed and intelligent position.

I agreed with the women in principle. I also understood the men's resistance. The military, particularly in the heat of battle, becomes archetypally collegial. War, a cut-throat contest to the point of dismemberment and death, is to the male mind clearly masculine. The discomfort and confusion of the men was due to their strong feeling about a masculine mystery they could not articulate, to say nothing of justify. The unspeakable subtext, I believe, was castration, the extremity of masculine annihilation. Including females in the mix puts a man's bones out of joint, but he can't exactly say why. How can a man argue what he deeply senses regarding collegiality?

Sometimes masculine collegiality is stereotypic, sometimes archetypal. In stereotypical situations, collegiality need not be maintained at all costs. In archetypal situations, it must, if damage is not to be done to masculine bonding and restoration. For this reason, girls did not belong in my teen-aged Boy Scout activities, with our naked wilderness swimming, joking about our growing genitals, the puberty initiations we concocted. None of these could have happened with girls present. Our own identities as males were too fragile and untested, our need for mutual affirmation too strong. There is a sense in which that kind of fragility remains throughout a man's life. Males need their own *temenos,* their own sacred space, even more urgently as traditionally sacred male precincts fall away. The more masculine collegiality is eroded, the more unreconstructed castrated males appear in our society.

In chapter three, I told of the theft of my wallet in Paris. When I arrived in Brussels, at the wrong station, in a forbidding industrial area, I hustled my heavy bags three blocks to the Hotel Continental, the neon sign for which was one of the few lights on that street. I told my sad story to the man at the desk, who turned out to be the owner. He gave me a bed, dinner, breakfast, two stiff belts of Scotch, a taxi voucher to the airport and $20, all without a credit card. The check I sent was not cashed. He sent me Christmas cards and an invitation to his wedding in Djakarta. He gave me *temenos* on the basis of collegiality. The same thing had happened to him in Toronto.

Sadness

In the videotape *A Gathering of Men,* Robert Bly speaks of the need for men to acknowledge and express grief. That there can be no mature masculinity without the inclusion of this acute sorrow may come to many men as something of a shock. Bly bases this necessity upon the missing or inadequate father. Grief, he says, grounds masculinity and becomes "the door to feeling" for a man. My immediate response was, "Of course."

Sadness might be a more inclusive, less dramatic way of expressing this necessity. The intensity of grief need not be present. A slow, gnawing awareness of loss, a lowering of spirits, dejection, sorrow, depression, are experiences every man has, whether or not sadness plunges into the abyss of grief. But why, when the nature of phallos is to be strong and imperturbable?

I can suggest three reasons related to castration.

The first is the separation from the mother as an essential precondition for the attainment of masculinity. Mother, archetypally, represents the human need for comfort, security, nourishment and affirming love—paradisical images a man must learn to live beyond. He cannot insist upon them without seriously compromising his hero's journey. A man has no right to mother-comfort beyond childhood. The ease he takes in his lifetime comes during and after hard work and hard love, in the midst of effort, not before. A lifetime of struggle carries with it a natural modicum of sadness. A man's loss of mother is a loss of what, as a child, he came to value and expect as integral to his sense of reality.

The second reason for sadness—perhaps grief is appropriate here—is a man's intimate experience with the psychological necessity of castration as a concomitant of his maleness. Since there is no way to avoid the castration issue—a male discovers this in his experiences of rejection—an element of sorrow is present in his emotional life from the outset. As has been noted, the paradoxical nature of castration requires that a man walk into the vortex of dismemberment in order fully to possess his masculine authority; avoidance only perpetuates self-doubt. This hardly brings unmitigated joy. The presence or potential of castration is sensed unconsciously by every male, no matter how it is described. Men who encounter serious depressive episodes in mid-life may well be those who have postponed, equivocated or compromised the psychological necessity of risking castration.

A third source of sadness for men comes from the nature of phallos even when it functions well. For a man both the excitement and the disappointment of living find their symbolic prototype in the behavior of his sexual organ: quiescence, inner urging, expansion, driving force, explosion and, inevitably, death. The phallic requirement is to stand up and be counted, then to fall into depletion and impotence, having spent its substance. Over time, this process has a melancholic effect on a man. A man's spirit is his phallic energy; it is spirit that triggers erection; it is spirit that pours forth in ejaculation. Spirit peaks and is gone. Phallos is exhausted A man tastes a morsel of the end.

To avoid sadness forces a man into an artificial posture, a pseudo-positive attitude that rings hollow. On the other hand, to embrace sadness and to allow the experience with gentle acceptance produces a seasoned wisdom that can evolve in no other way. If the carrying of sadness is evaded, it can emerge as despair—an exaggeration of a natural sadness, enormously compacted by denial. This is sadness at its nadir.

Bly's inclusion of grief as an essential requirement of masculinity is sobering and compelling. I remember a colleague's devastating comment on a fellow analyst: "He has not suffered." Once said, I knew its truth. A look of sadness, bespeaking untold suffering, reveals a spiritual attitude gained only through the embrace of loss, a movement away from triumph, finesse, manner, callow sureness and established command. Sadness undercuts patriarchal presumption at every hand; it does not live well with obsessive domination. Sadness may in fact be the primary bonding element in meetings between adult men. And while phallic attainment is a source of male-male admiration (as well as competition), sadness might be the source of male gentleness and kindness toward one another.

Respect

Respect has to do with honoring, with honoring oneself, with esteemed regard. It is not the same as admiration. Admiration has to do with wonder; men wonder at phallos, at another man's phallic capacity. Yet admiration and respect are related. I would say that respect is vintage admiration, that admiration precedes respect, that respect is mellow and nicely aged. Admiration has the seed of envy, even desire. It is youthful, hungry, wanting more.

One can genuinely respect another only when one first respects oneself. The need for self-respect is urgent for any man, the more so as he bears within him still open wounds from the injuries of castration. Self-respect grows when a man becomes willing to wait for phallos to reappear, finding a growing confidence that insult and injury can be borne, that permanent damage has not been done. He does not then have to borrow from another man to redress his deficiency, much less steal or destroy. A vindictive man must wonder if his self-respect is in trouble. A pocket of self-doubt may be touched, a pocket filled with dynamite, ready to explode, a displacement of genuine phallic energy into emotional volatility.

Other-respect is a test of self-respect. A man unsure of himself should ask some questions. What men do I respect, not admire or envy, but respect? Do I actually respect any man? How do I show it? Do I find myself unwilling to offer respect to respectable men? Do I have any idea why I have a stingy reluctance to offer recognition to men of quality? Does this reflect an attitude toward myself?

A man will never find himself totally free of obsequious admiration. In some part of himself he will swerve toward envy, as though another man were always better, more accomplished, more masculine, more phallic. Castration anxiety—in ground-in chronic situations, the complex—makes itself felt as on-going desire. Desire may not focus upon the other man's body (although one sometimes gets that impression considering the enormous amount of time men spend watching young athletes), but upon the other man's attainments—his wealth, fortitude, leadership, influence. Envy is a disguised form of sexual desire. One wants what the other owns, which psychologically translates as his phallic presence. Men know that in locker rooms it is impossible not to be aware of the nakedness of others even if one resists the impulse to look. Comparison is intrinsic to masculinity; envy always lurks in the nooks and crannies of a man's unconscious.

Respect moves beyond comparison—the higher/longer the other man, the lower/shorter the admirer. Respect cuts through the round of covetousness, obsessive measuring, always having to beat the other guy. The remarkable factor allowing respect is a man's inner knowledge that masculine penis envy is no longer the issue it once was. A man able to respect another man is confident of his masculine grid, warts and all. He is proud of himself and he is able to share his pride with an honorable brother.

Phallos is not thereby disregarded. On the contrary, phallos as prototype of masculinity finds distinguished expression in the celebration of another man. This is mature narcissism, the full round from Freud's infantile sexuality.

Deconstruction

Deconstruction is a current philosophical/linguistic movement that is congruent with an aspect of feminist thought. Deconstructionism aims to deinstitutionalize reason, law and especially language. By refusing fixed meaning, the immutability and timelessness of signs, whether verbal or spatial, deconstructionists attack patriarchal design. Deconstructionism turns a text reflexively against itself, seeking the fantasy hidden in a language that manifests itself outwardly, in the male-dominated world, as doctrine. The position of the reader/viewer is not determined by traditional meaning. The "text" and reader are seen as interactive; both are subjects.

Deconstructionism's emphasis on relativity balances the overconstruction of patriarchy, which has dominated the structure and use of language and sign in Western civilization. Overconstruction is clearly superpatriarchal; it shows itself to be psychologically priapic in its insistence upon outer activity and external accomplishment as a substantiation of superiority.

Deconstructionism may be a subjective step toward dismantling patriarchy. It edges the scrim from patriarchal eyes, blinded by a tradition based upon power based upon fear, whether expressed by males or females. Jungian psychology, drawing as it does upon inner authority, is both premodern and postmodern (deconstructionist), since it takes interiority as the final arbiter of authenticity. Its inner viewpoint is prescientific (romantic as opposed to rational) and postscientific (soulful as opposed to empirical). In its focus upon interiority, it has from its outset called into question the overconstructed collective structures of consciousness.

For a man to deconstruct means almost literally to pull apart his patriarchal house, beam by beam, maybe even splinter by splinter. In doing so, he will discover a reality much deeper than his political structuring, his satisfaction in managing and calling the shots for those in his supposed domain. Since patriarchy is a covering for castration, deconstruction exposes castration as the energy behind rule. Patriarchy is a splint, but the broken bone beneath is never acknowledged. Instead the old king hobbles, wondering why his kingdom is sick at its core.

Deconstruction is not reconstruction. Phallos is not reconstructed. It is revivified. The other night my wife and I had a talk about Christmas. Barbara told me that she wanted to attend service at the Church of the Epiphany, where she went to Sunday school, just around the back-40 from our house. Our family belongs to St. Luke's in downtown Scranton, some fifteen miles away. I believe in downtowns; I have worked hard at St. Luke's, spending myself in its behalf. I have no emotional connection with Epiphany Church. I fancy midnight mass, its power and its glory. I love the long drive down and back in the middle of the night and take pride in our family's filling up a pew. Barbara chose the 7:00 p.m. Christmas eve eucharist at Epiphany. She is tired late at night. She feels no allegiance to St. Luke's. She prefers country to cathedral. Furthermore, I'd had my way for thirty years, in New York, in Zurich, in Scranton. I am a priest, and Christmas is my religious neighborhood. It seemed time for me to deconstruct.

These six antidotes—mentoring, touching, collegiality, sadness, respect and deconstruction—by no means exhaust the possibilities for redemption of a man's phallic prowess and pride from the labyrinth of castration. One could mention also such elementary masculine behaviors as fathering, focusing, perseverance, awakening to instinct, to name only a few. The essential thing for a man with a castration problem is to act, to move away from the stasis binding him to his wound.

The character of masculinity is naturally extraverted, since the organ of gender is exterior to the body, always pointed toward an object. Yet there is a paradoxical aspect to castration remedy, moving as it does from the gender-specific externality of masculinity into a deeply subjective, and thus introverted, re-forming of phallos. The masculine grid is the intrapsychic, thus interior, foundation for a man's exterior phallic functioning, even as exterior phallos characterizes the interior structure. For a man to move his frame of reference within is itself a kind of doing, very different from feminine being.

Erection that is lost from ejaculation returns, as spirit reinvigorates the masculine grid. Spirit comes from within. A man's turn-on is inspired by an external person, but the source is his internal image system. His phallic action is without exception always extraverted, penetrating, magnetically drawn toward an object. The foundation of that action is, however, interior—deeply grounded within the structure of his unconscious. An inner psychic process is required for erection to reoccur. This dynamic seems to put erectile resurgence into the hands of the anima, the soul, the contrasexual feminine.

For a man to get close to another man, to depend upon a mentor, to touch, to claim another as brother, to allow sadness, to offer respect, involves an awareness of need, a curiosity about soul, a desire to tie into an inner aspect that seems antithetical to outward phallic stability and prowess. Indeed it is, and yet it isn't, and yet it is. Such a condition is not only paradoxical, it is paradox doubled. The ability to confess need stems from the same inner dynamic that produces erection—the anima.

Manliness requires male patterning. It may also be that the impetus for all masculine grid-building is feminine, whether a man finds himself sexually drawn to males or females or both. Interiority, obscure to the male, is the starting place of renewed erection; need, so foreign to patriarchy, is indigenous to phallos.

5
Epilogue: Masthead Reborn

The original depiction of castration in Greek mythology, and in the lore of the West, is the story of Ouranos (Uranus), Father Sky, who was partner to Gaia, Earth Mother. Of their union were born the Titans, the Cyclopes and, finally, three monsters.

With the first brood, Ouranos dealt harshly: he is variously reported to have stuffed them back into Gaia's womb or shut them up in the depths of the earth, which mythologically amounts to the same thing. His motivation may have been his desire for Gaia's entire attention as well as the protection of his reign. Gaia detested Ouranos; she sought revenge, and freedom for her children.

The last-born of the Titans, Cronos, came to his mother's aid. Cronos said, "I too loathe my father. I will help you."

> As dark night and Ouranos descended on her bedchamber, Gaia lay sighing erotically and stroking the bed beside her. Ouranos's whole anatomy responded. He bounded into the bedchamber fully erect.
>
> Cronos lunged forward, out of hiding, and seized his father's mastodonic member with his left hand and with his right brought down the jagged flint sickle Gaia had fashioned for the occasion.
>
> Immortally wounded, Ouranos whispered the prophecy that would be his son's demise, "Exult not, as you have done to me, so your son shall do to you." His father's blood dripping from his hands, Cronos turned to his mother. Her eyes confirmed the truth.[87]

Ancient and deep are the wellsprings of castration. The tale of Ouranos, Gaia and Cronos is so old and its elements are so basic to life that the father has given his name to the heavens, the mother to earth, the son to time. The roots of Western civilization come from

---

[87] Donald Richardson, *Great Zeus and All His Children* (quoted by Makwa in "Beware of Empty Vessels," *Wingspan,* Spring 1990, p. 9).

Greece, and the Greeks knew this myth as their original story.

The very suggestion of castration creates such discomfort in men, it is so horrific an element of masculine life, that the subject can even be avoided in psychotherapy. In mythology, the drama is clear; in ordinary life its devastating prologue and ensuing panoramic consequences may be obscure, since they move into metaphor and implication. Yet men in analysis repeat variations of the Ouranos tale. The jealousy of the father, the one-step-removed hand of the mother's retribution, masked behind her sighing and stroking, the son's hatred and vicious defense of his mother, are common. The threads of the story weave together to an inevitable conclusion in masculine psychology. If one is to get a man, castration is the way.

The evil prophecy the cut-down father makes about his son's future works itself out in life after life. Cronos, in turn, to prevent his own castration, devoured his children by Rhea. Except for the last, Zeus. Rhea finally outwitted Cronos after her delivery. Cronos must have been a klutz, for he mistakenly swallowed a rock instead of Zeus, and lived out his life as a duped man, full of stony intransigence. Ouranos' prophecy sets the stage for Cronos'—and everyman's—lifelong struggle to maintain himself within a vortex of castration analogues, caught up in battles he is called upon to win but can win only by involving himself in a new round of diminishment.

Zeus, following the pattern, vanquished his father. "Cronos was driven from the sky and cast to the very depths of the universe and there enchained in the region which stretches beneath the earth and the fruitless sea."[88]

Ouranos and Cronos, devastating and devastated, and Zeus, now in his prime, tell the male fate, underlined, overlined, by godly example. Being cut off, duped, responding to one's baleful ignorance by stony intransigence, is a masculine nightmare. Entering doom, stealthfully enticed by a female patting the bed, makes a man the fool that he fears he is. A woman might protest that the curse began with Ouranos' denial of their children, his potential competitors, but

---

[88] *New Larousse Encyclopedia of Mythology,* p. 91.

blame does not alleviate the problem.

Being "enchained in the region which stretches beneath the earth and the fruitless sea" is mythic language for the experience of discouraged and debilitated men. They can't move. Their seed, ceaselessly made, inseminates no one. The world in which they lie is dark; the seed is as though it were not there; the sea—might that be the seminal fluid?—is fruitless. Men dig in for the duration, walled off in defiance, demanding in steely silence that they be recognized and respected. There can be no recognition or respect without The Presence. In castration, The Presence is gone.

Not all the effects of castration can be reversed; the injury is often profound and forever marks a man's life, propelling him into the myth. The victim can be, as was Ouranos, "immortally wounded," his godlike quality gone. Men do go on, bearing the injury, but it is a sad and stolid journey. Psychoanalysis is often hoped for as cure. It is not, if cure is understood as the abolition of a condition. Therapy is the discovery of what is, and the learning to live with it.

Every man must learn to live with castration. Recently, once again, I was flying into what is officially called the Wilkes-Barre/Scranton International Airport. Once again, I was told what the temperature was in Wilkes-Barre, welcomed to Wilkes-Barre, etc., etc., even as I was flying over downtown Scranton on our final approach. Scranton had the idea for a joint airport (Wilkes-Barre is fifteen miles away), is forty per cent larger and comes first alphabetically. The airport is on Scranton's city limits. Yet Wilkes-Barre would cooperate only if its name came first. So Scranton is called, by air personnel in a hurry, Wilkes-Barre. My rationalizations are flawless. My protests change nothing. It drives me just a little bit nuts.

I know I have something of a problem here. Some part of me is psychologically identified with Scranton. When Scranton is ignored, I feel myself ignored; it might not go too far to say impotent. I have come to recognize this strange state of affairs as the product of my castration complex: I take personal offense at what other people hardly notice. This glitch of neurosis will not go away; it probably is stuck onto me for good. I can mentally work on my obsession, but I know it will come up each time I fly home. But I do have to stop talking about it at dinner parties with people from Wilkes-Barre. It's too damn boring.

It helps if I rehearse my complex when I walk on the plane in Pittsburgh. It also helps when I do something concrete for Scranton, like serving on boards; this gets the thing out of my head. It helps me to get connected to a more important issue, to nudge my complex aside when it gets just too ridiculous. It used to be that I was terrified of flying; analysis helped me with that. Maybe my complex has become downwardly mobile. Scranton is a smaller problem than death, if I've got to worry about something. And I do try to remember that phallos is honored even in injury. My idiosyncrasy points to a much greater mystery that impinges on every man when he hits a wobble in his grid.

Was castration handled in the myth? There are possibilities. From the severed genitalia of Ouranos, cast into the sea, sprang forth white foam from which was born the goddess of love, Aphrodite herself. In other versions of the story, Cronos, the son/castrator, "was sent to the ends of the earth to dwell in bliss, or plunged into mysterious slumber in distant Thule."[89] Mysterious slumber, even bliss at the ends of the earth, may be a questionable solution. Treatment that promises paradise contradicts itself, since phallos and castration have a necessary paradoxical requirement for one another. The goddess of love issuing from Ouranos' severed member says that no bad thing is only bad. Castration and creation, castration and love, can find a way to coexist.

The castration saga, finally, has religious meaning. The depth of fear and rage in Ouranos, the depth of maternal protection in Gaia, the depth of vengeance in Cronos, permit no facile textbook medication. A father despised his offspring; a mother fashioned the dagger of destruction for her husband; a son severed the source of his own generation. Gods have no exemption from evil and suffering. In our own loss, our "immortal wounding," we edge close, or closer, to

---

[89] Ibid.

being godlike. That, I take it, is the point of mythic tragedy. The mystery of love and hate between husband, wife and child is a tangle of truth and falsehood. Escape is often at the cost of a burial under an artificial somnolent bliss.

Religious meaning, as understood by Jung, is psychological meaning. To the popular mind, religion signifies an answer that makes things more comfortable and morally correct; it is almost always associated with religious organizations and their dogmas. Jung, however, knew *religio* in its ancient sense: "to go through again, to think over, to recollect . . . . to reconnect, link back."[90] As such, religion is the work of soul-searching, of digging into one's personal history, dreams and conflicts, and the world's, as the way to the gods. Even my weirdness about Scranton has religious meaning. I find myself damaged and needy. When I delve into my projection upon place, I discover a truth about myself.

A man's personal tragedy becomes not so strange to him when he learns that a god lived out a similar fate. Men seem, to themselves and to others, gullibly caught in an inescapable net of circumstance, driven by fleeting and undependable instinct. The more they do, the less permanence they find. Like Ouranos, they head stupidly into the fray, high on phallic prowess, only to be cut down, a variation of impotence. Efforts to improve things make matters worse. Power ends as weakness. They are chaff; the kernel is elsewhere.

This work is a reconsideration of an ancient religious issue that has become a cliché. Freud set the stage; his consideration of castration was limited by his concentration upon childhood trauma. Jung extended Freud into the vast realm of the collective unconscious, but did not explore castration as such. Since then, Jungians have done nothing that I have found to move Freud's enormous contribution into the milieu of analytical psychology. For men, and for those who love them, the issue is too important to be sidestepped, left behind in moldering tomes of psychoanalytic theory. Phallos and its wounding are coincident with masculinity. Patriarchy served a purpose in

---

[90] *Symbols of Transformation,* par. 669.

providing needed structures to the Western world. Now it is deservedly creaking in its bones and men need to find a new sense of self-definition.

Recently in Tucson, after my lecture ("Phallos: Alternative to Patriarchy") a woman rose to ask whether I realized that a substantial amount of the language I used in decrying patriarchy was itself patriarchal. I took a breath, told myself that the question was not hostile—which it wasn't then and never became—and then remembered something. In editing another work with my associate, Alice Petersen, she flagged a word commonly used in analytical psychology, so commonly that one hardly thinks about its implication as it tumbles out of the mental storehouse. "You can't use *anthropos,*" said Alice. I knew immediately what she meant, though I was impatient at what I experienced as yet another feminist intrusion. *Anthropos* is Greek for man. It was long used in alchemical writing as the original image of mankind (which in those days included women) in the primal psyche. Jung gave it currency; it means something to a Jungian audience. No one even thinks about its etymology. Alice did.

I told that story to my Tucson audience. I also said that often I offer a caveat or two at the start of my presentations indicating my awareness of the difficulty presented by our common tongue regarding both sexist and heterosexual presumptions and prejudices. I had not that evening.

Frankly, I sometimes grow weary of the constant necessity in today's world to explain and defend vocabulary, to weed out potentially offensive terminology, to expand examples to include everybody. I use heterosexual paradigms because I am familiar with them, because translating everything into a syntax acceptable to gay men would convolute my thinking and engage me in a language and thought process that I don't use. Sexist language and thought structures are built into the way we talk and write. I know that I falter on the path of deconstruction, that what I am doing doesn't work as it once might have, and that it shouldn't. It's a feeble excuse and I don't defend it.

What Alice and I did on that editing day was stop and, once I had calmed down, browse through our heads for an alternative to *anthropos*. First we left the English language, as an aid to innovation. Then we ranged around for a base-word that included both genders and was recognizable. In German and English, *person* is the same. The prefix *ur* had exactly the meaning I needed: primal, original, source. So we made up a new word, new at least to us and to the dictionaries at our disposal. *Urperson* (ur'-per-sohn) has none of the patriarchal etymology of *anthropos*. Of course, it has none of the tradition either, but we wondered if in use over time it could become as recognizable to English speakers as are, say, ego, psyche, libido, etc.

Something like this process will be necessary if our language and thought structures are to represent and reflect our new consciousness. The work may be tiresome, but the sense of freedom from restrictive metaphor is liberating and delightful. In a way, it is not unlike the repair of masculine injury. Nothing happens if the old stuff is simply repeated, if the trouble is not noted or if the pointing out is rejected. The man who knows that the need for change in patriarchal language bodes no ill for his phallic identity is prepared, at the basic level, to enter an exciting renewal. Still, my lack of patience with Alice points to the difficulty men have in surrendering their traditional prerogatives. Prerogative in Western society means patriarchy. Phallos does not mean prerogative.

Mihaly Csikszentmihalyi of the University of Chicago asks in his review of Robert Bly's *Iron John: A Book About Men*:

> After all, why assume that the two genders need different myths, or that women can't initiate boys into manhood? Why not assume a generic human psyche, and unisex role models? . . . Four million years in which men and women prospered by maximizing complementary characteristics, eons that etched different patterns on the neural networks of the two genders, cannot—with all the good will in the world—be erased in a few decades. Nor can the subtle tendrils of culture, which entangle us in traditional gender roles, be cut without running the risk of bleeding the sap out of a growing man, or woman.[91]

---

[91] "Bring on the Hairy Mentor," p. 16.

Epilogue: Masthead Reborn 133

Bleeding the sap of a growing man, or of any male, is what I have called castration. As the reader knows by now, I believe that the execution or foreboding of phallic erasure, writ large or small in a male's psychology, is precisely the source of his worry about bleeding and his defense against it. It is little helped by speculation that the biological and psychological characteristics of masculinity have no reflexive relationship. Even less does alleviation come by ignoring the depth of connection between a man's body and his soul. The collapse of patriarchy leaves no traditional base upon which men can understand themselves. The starting place is with a man's proudest possession.

Men can take heart. The sap can flow again.

One man went a fitful way for forty years before he found his art, then moved to a place which was a center of that art, but could not quickly find a way in. He started at the bottom once again, and spent weeks in semidepression, a testimony to his discovery, then loss, of personal prowess. Examining his low, he found that his anguish was indeed related to his sense of pride in himself: his courage, his sacrifice, his obedience to an inner Presence. One could say that he suffered, but he had found his cock.

Another man was terrified that two visits to prostitutes had infected him with the AIDS virus and that he might pass it on to his wife and child. He lacerated himself, full of guilt and self-loathing, for having briefly jumped out of line with his wild side. Through analytic work he came to respect that part of himself that was not, and never would be, "good."

Yet another man felt that his love of sexuality was a flaw, incompatible with his love of spirit—that his body pleasure had to go. After some attention to this split, he began to glimpse their profound connection, that he need not cut himself off from chthonic pleasure to find enlightenment, that phallos leads to ecstasy and that ecstasy is entering the transpersonal.

I could give forty stories.

And then there are the women who love phallos and testes and celebrate them. They entice erection, experiencing an outer manifesta-

134 Epilogue: Masthead Reborn

tion of an inner secret. I have recently found two poets of this ilk. (A man always hopes to meet such a woman, whose delight and surprise confirm and cooperate with his inner realization.) One is Anne MacNaughton. She writes for women with a salty sense of humor that I love, in a poem called "Teste Moanial":

> Actually, it's the balls I look for, always.
> Men in the street, offices, cars, restaurants.
> it's the nuts I imagine—
> firm, soft, in hairy sacks
> the way they are
> down there rigged between the thighs,
> the funny way they are.
> One in front, a little in front of the other,
> slightly higher. The way they slip
> between your fingers, the way they
> slip around in their soft sack.
> The way they swing when he walks,
> hang down when he bends
> over. You see them sometimes bright pink
> out of a pair of shorts
> when he sits wide and unaware,
> the hair sparse and wiry
> like that on a poland china pig.
> You can see the skin right through—speckled,
> with wrinkles like a prune, but loose,
> slipping over those kernals
> rocking the smooth, small huevos.
> So delicate, the cock becomes a diversion,
> a masthead overlarge, its flag distracting
> from beautiful pebbles beneath.[92]

Less phallos, that, than a testament to the gentleness of scrotum as half the masculine system. Not exactly the way a man sees himself, but deliciously connected as a woman gives the message. Symbolic power, joined with feminine wonder, biologically, is a way into a man's discovery of himself.

---

[92] In Donald Hall, ed., *Best American Poetry 1989*.

The other poet is Sharon Olds, who celebrates the Presence, the essence of phallos, in "The Connoisseuse of Slugs."

> When I was a connoisseuse of slugs
> I would part the ivy leaves, and look for the
> naked jelly of those gold bodies,
> translucent strangers glistening along the
> stones, slowly, their gelatinous bodies
> at my mercy. Mostly made of water, they would shrivel
> to nothing if they were sprinkled with salt,
> but I was not interested in that. What I liked
> was to draw aside the ivy, breathe the
> odor of the wall, and stand there in silence
> until the slug forgot I was there
> and sent its antennae up out of its
> head, the glimmering umber horns
> like rising telescopes, until finally the
> sensitive knobs would pop out the ends,
> delicate and intimate. Years later,
> when I first saw a naked man,
> I gasped with pleasure to see that quiet
> mystery reenacted, the slow
> elegant being coming out of hiding and
> gleaming in the dark air, eager and so
> trusting you could weep.[93]

When there are folk like that, phallos springs back, castration be damned. Sharon Olds writes in another poem, in celebration after she and her husband made love, "I have never seen a happier man."[94]

His god-member worked well.

---

[93] *The Dead and the Living,* p. 51.
[94] Ibid., p. 56.

Bibliography

Bataille, Georges. *Erotism: Death and Sensuality.* Trans. Mary Dalwood. San Francisco: City Lights, 1986.

Bly, Robert. *Iron John: A Book About Men.* Reading, MA: Addison-Wesley Publishing Co., 1990.

Bly, Robert, and Moyers, Bill. *A Gathering of Men.* Videotape. Produced by Public Affairs Television, Inc., 1990.

Boss, Medard. *Psychoanalysis and Daseinanalysis.* Trans. Ludwig B. Lefebre. New York: Basic Books, Inc., 1963.

Burns, Ken, producer/director. *The Civil War.* Film series produced by Florentine Films and WETA-TV (Public Broadcasting System), 1990.

Campbell, Joseph. *Transformations of Myth Through Time.* New York: Harper & Row, 1990.

Csikszentmihalyi, Mihaly. "Bring on the Hairy Mentor." In *New York Times Book Review,* December 9, 1990.

deWicce, Patrikyia. "A Soft and Gentle Paw." In *Changing Men,* Spring/Summer 1988.

Dinesen, Isak (Karen Blixen). *Out of Africa.* New York: Random House (Modern Library edition), 1952.

Freud, Sigmund. *The Standard Edition of the Complete Psychological Works of Sigmund Freud.* Ed. J. Strachey, A. Freud. London: Hogarth Press, 1961.

Gould, Stephen Jay. *Ontogeny and Phylogeny.* Cambridge: Harvard University Press, 1977.

Harrison, Sue. *Mother Earth, Father Sky.* New York: Doubleday, 1990.

Hall, Donald, ed. *Best American Poetry 1989.* New York: Macmillan & Co., 1989.

Horney, Karen. *Feminine Psychology.* Ed. and with an Introduction by Harold Kelman. New York: W.W. Norton & Co., 1967.

Jaffé, Aniela, ed. *C.G. Jung: Word and Image* (Bollingen Series XCVII:2). Princeton: Princeton University Press, 1979.

Johnson, Robert. *Ecstasy: Understanding the Psychology of Joy.* San Francisco: Harper & Row, 1989.

Jung, C.G. *The Collected Works* (Bollingen Series XX). 20 vols. Trans. R.F.C. Hull. Ed. H. Read, M. Fordham, G. Adler, Wm. McGuire. Princeton: Princeton University Press, 1953-1979.

———. *Memories, Dreams, Reflections*. Trans. Richard and Clara Winston. Ed. Aniela Jaffé. New York: Pantheon Books, 1963.

——— (quoted). *The Wisdom of the Dream* (vol. 1: "A Life of Dreams"). Videotape. Border Television/Stephen Segaller Films, 1989.

Kinsley, David. *The Sword and the Flute: Kali and Krsna, Dark Visions of the Terrible and the Sublime in Hindu Mythology*. Berkeley: University of California Press, 1975.

Klein, Melanie. *The Selected Melanie Klein*. Ed. Juliet Mitchell. New York: Free Press, 1986.

Kohut, Heinz. *The Analysis of the Self: A Systematic Approach to the Psychoanalytic Treatment of Narcissistic Personality Disorders*. New York: International Universities Press, 1977.

———. *How Does Analysis Cure?* Chicago: University of Chicago Press, 1984.

———. *The Restoration of the Self*. New York: International Universities Press, 1977.

Kovel, Joel. *The Age of Desire: Reflections of a Radical Psychoanalyst*. New York: Pantheon Books, 1981.

Martin, Stephen. "Anger As Inner Transformation." In *Quadrant*, vol. 19, no. 1 (Spring 1986).

Miller, David. "World Peace: The Influence of the Unconscious." Paper presented at the First Scranton Conference on Jungian Psychology and Social Issues, University of Scranton, June 1990.

Money, John, and Ehrhardt, Anke A. *Man and Woman, Boy and Girl*. Baltimore: Johns Hopkins Press, 1972.

Monick, Eugene. *Phallos: Sacred Image of the Masculine*. Toronto: Inner City Books, 1987.

Neumann, Erich. *The Great Mother: An Analysis of the Archetype* (Bollingen Series XLVII). Trans. Ralph Manheim. Princeton: Princeton University Press, 1972.

———. *The Origins and History of Consciousness* (Bollingen Series XLII). Trans. R.F.C. Hull. Princeton: Princeton University Press, 1970.

New Larousse Encyclopedia of Mythology. London: Hamlyn, 1968.

Olds, Sharon. *The Dead and the Living.* New York: Alfred A. Knopf, 1990.

Onians, R.B. *The Origins of European Thought about the Body, the Mind, the Soul, the World, Time, and Fate.* Reprint of the 1951 ed. New York: Arno Press, 1973.

Paglia, Camille. *Sexual Personae: Art and Decadence from Nefertiti to Emily Dickenson.* New Haven, CT: Yale University Press, 1990.

Palmer, George Herbert, trans. *The Odyssey of Homer.* New York: Houghton, Mifflin & Co., 1891.

Reis, Patricia. "The Mysteries of Creativity: Self-Seeding, Death, and the Great Goddess." In *Psychological Perspectives,* vol. 17, no. 1 (Spring 1986).

Richardson, Donald. *Great Zeus and All His Children.* New York: Prentice-Hall, 1984.

Samuels, Andrew, et al. *A Critical Dictionary of Jungian Analysis.* New York: Routledge & Kegan Paul, 1987.

Sharp, Daryl. *The Survival Papers: Anatomy of a Midlife Crisis.* Toronto: Inner City Books, 1988.

_____. *Jung Lexicon: A Primer of Terms and Concepts.* Toronto: Inner City Books, 1991.

Swedish Television. *The Miracle of Life.* Public Broadcasting System (U.S.), NOVA series, 1986.

Wallis, Brian, ed. *Art After Modernism: Rethinking Representation.* Boston: The New Museum of Contemporary Art, New York, and David R. Godine, 1984.

Wyly, James. *The Phallic Quest: Priapus and Masculine Inflation.* Toronto: Inner City Books, 1989.

Index

accomplishment, 29-32
additionality, 24
Adler, Alfred, 62
adolescence, 29-30, 65
Adonis, 86
aggression, 74
AIDS, 72, 133
alchemy, 19, 36, 106, 111, 131
analysis, Jungian, 33-34, 128
Analysis of the Self, 52
androcentrism, 22, 41
anger, 9, 98-99
anima, 34-36, 60-65, 72, 76, 103
animus, 15n
anthropos, 131-132
antidotes, to castration:
   collegiality, 117-119
   deconstruction, 123-125
   mentoring, 112-114
   respect, 121-123
   sadness, 119-121
   touching, 114-117
anxiety, 23, 25, 42-43, 49-50, 53, 57, 78-98, 122
Aphrodite, 99-100, 129
archetype(s)/archetypal: 9-12, 19-20, 26-28, 44, 52, 57-59, 63, 66, 69, 74-75, 78-79, 90, 95, 111-112
   and instinct, 10, 12, 19, 28, 44
   and stereotype, 23, 119
Ares, 99-100
Astarte, 86
Attis, 8, 86-87, 89
auto-castration, 86-89

Bataille, Georges, 115
being, versus doing, 25, 30, 51, 112

Binswanger, Ludwig, 96
bisexuality, 47-48, 63, 79
black men, 90-92
Bly, Robert, 114, 119-121, 132
brooding, 69
Brünhilde, 61-62
Burns, Ken, 68
Bush, George, 81, 83, 110n

Campbell, Joseph, 107
Campeau, Robert, 110
Carter, Jimmy, 81-82
castration: 10-15 and passim
   and animus, 15n
   antidotes to, 90, 112-125
   anxiety, 23, 25, 42-43, 49-50, 53, 57, 78-98, 122
   auto-, 86-89
   complex, 49-50, 54
   by fate, 93-96
   female-male, 83-86, 105
   and femininity, 14, 17, 23-24, 31, 54, 58, 67, 78-80
   Freud's views, 39-49, 79-80
   Jung's views, 55-66, 79-80
   male-male, 79-83
   ontological, 96-98
   paradox of, 104-107
   patriarchal, 91-92
   psychological meaning, 10-11, 17
   as rejection, 45
   signs of, 108-112
   societal, 89-93
   symbolic, 44-48, 51, 57-66
celibacy, 18, 88-89
chance, 94-96
childbirth, 74
childhood sexuality, 25-29, 39-48
Christ, 19, 88-89

139

chthonic, 9n, 10, 14, 16, 36, 91, 115-116
circularity, 21, 55
circumcision, 15n, 74-75
Civil War, The, 68
clitoris, 24, 40-41
collegiality, 117-119
competition, 81, 117-118, 121
complex, 49-50, 60, 63, 128-129
coniunctio oppositorum, 19
"Connoisseuse of Slugs, The," 135
courage, 70
creativity, 18-19, 30-31, 129
creature anxiety, 50
Cronos, 126-129
Csikszentmihalyi, Mihaly, 132
curiosity, 29-30
Cybele, 86-87

Daseinanalysis, 50, 96-97
Dead Poets' Society, 87
debauchery, 92
deconstruction, 92, 123-125, 131-132
developmental psychology, 56-57
deWicce, Patricia, 17-18
Dinesen, Isak, 36-37
doing, versus being, 25, 30, 51, 112, 125
"Dread of Woman, The," 12
dream(s): of dismemberment, 106
of intimacy, 117
penis in, 21-22
of plowing earth, 22
"Dual Mother, The," 59
Dukakis, Michael, 81-82

"Early Stages of the Oedipal Conflict," 61
ecstasy, 17, 19, 30-31, 133
ego: as hero, 57-59, 65
seduction of, 31
Ehrhardt, Anke, 25-26, 28
Eliade, Mircea, 9

emotion, 67-68, 103, 108-109
enantiodromia, 74
envy, 122
eros, 40, 75, 116
Erotism: Death and Sensuality, 115
eucharist, 19
eunuch, 88-89

fate, 93-96
Fates, three, 95-96
father, 27-30, 43-48, 57, 80-81, 91-92, 112-115, 126-129
Faust, 24
feeling, 66-67, 102-103
female-male castration, 83-86
feminine/femininity: 10-12, 14, 21, 23-25, 27, 29, 34-37, 50-52, 54-56, 58-81, 95-96, 112, 125
and being, 25, 30, 51
brooding, 69
"female" work, 75
integration of, 34-35, 66-77, 103
repudiation of, 54, 79-80
Feminine Psychology, 50
feminism, 72-73, 84
Freud, Sigmund, 13-15, 19, 23-26, 28-29, 39-60, 79-80, 92, 96-97, 99, 123, 130

Gathering of Men, A, 119
gender identity/differentiation, 11-12, 16-20, 22-31, 45-48, 53, 59
genital stage, 40
Goethe, 24
Gould, Stephen Jay, 56
Great Mother, 88-89, 91
grid: masculine, 14, 20-23, 36-38, 46, 48, 63, 74, 89, 99, 125
patriarchal, 22-23
grief, 119-121
guilt, 87-88

Harrison, Sue, 73
Heidegger, Martin, 96

Helms, Senator Jesse, 90
Hephaestus, 99-100
Heraclitus, 74
hero, 15n, 57-59, 62-66, 74, 80, 102
hierophany, 9
hieros gamos, 36, 77
homoeroticism, 71-72
Horney, Karen, 12-13, 30-31, 50-54, 60-62, 80
humiliation, 82-83

identification, 43-48, 57
impotence, 18, 31, 33, 61-64
incest, 29, 43-48, 60, 112
individuation, 28-29, 32-38, 57, 59-77, 99
indolence, 63
infantile sexuality, 25-28, 39-42, 59, 99, 123
initiation, 112-113
inner marriage, 36
instinct, and archetype, 10, 12, 19, 28, 44, 65, 91
integration, of the feminine, 34-35, 66-77, 103
intimacy, 116-117
introversion, 29, 36
Iron John: A Book About Men, 132
irrationality, 14
Ishtar, 86

Johnson, Robert, 116
Jung, C.G., 8, 9n, 10, 14-19, 24, 29, 33-34, 36, 41, 53-65, 74, 79-80, 87, 89, 92, 94-98, 106-107, 111, 116, 130-131

Kali, 106-107
Kelman, Harold, 30, 50
Kinsley, David, 107
Klein, Melanie, 61
Kohut, Heinz, 26, 50, 52-54
Kovel, Joel, 52

latency, 29-30, 45-48, 57, 63
libido, 17-20, 29-30, 40-41, 47-48
logos, 50
logos spermatikos, 111
looking, 56

MacNaughton, Anne, 134
male-male castration, 79-83
marriage, inner, 36
Martin, Stephen, 98-99
masculine/masculinity: and additionality, 24
and anxiety, 23, 25, 42-43, 49-50
and doing, 25, 30, 51
and gender identity, 11-12, 16-20, 22-23, 25-31
grid, 14, 20-23, 36-38, 46, 48, 63, 74, 89, 99, 125
protest, 62
stages of, 23-38
and transformation, 16-38, 57-59
masochism, 51
masturbation, 25, 27, 42-43, 47, 115
matriarchal, 26
mentoring, 112-114
mid-life crisis, 32-33
Milken, Michael, 110
Miller, David, 23
Miracle of Life, The, 94
mirroring, 13, 26-27, 43, 52-53, 59
Mississippi Burning, 81-82
Money, John, 25-26, 28
mother, 26-29, 32, 35, 37, 41-48, 50-52, 54, 59, 63-66, 69, 78, 83-85, 88-89, 91-92, 105, 112, 120, 126-129

narcissism, 32, 47, 52-53, 59, 123
Neumann, Erich, 26, 30, 91-92
neurosis, 71, 81, 128-129
Newman, Deanne, 22-23
Norns, 95
numinosity, 24, 55

142 Index

Odysseus, 100-101
oedipal: conflict/drama, 41-48, 80, 112
  stage, 28-29, 41-48, 53, 63, 74
Oedipus myth, 42-44
Olds, Sharon, 135
ontological castration, 96-98
opposites, union of, 19, 36
Origen, 89
Osiris, 107
Ouranos, 126-129
Out of Africa, 36-37
overconstruction, 109-112, 123-124

Paglia, Camille, 69n
paradox, 58, 104-107, 120
passivity, 54, 79-80
patriarchy/patriarchal: 9-11, 22-23, 35, 54, 66, 79, 82, 90-92, 105, 110n, 121, 123-125, 130-132
  castration, 91-92
  design, 14, 38
Pelle, the Conqueror, 85
penis: 24-26, 28, 40-43, 47, 51
  in dream, 21-22
  -envy, 40-41, 50-51, 54
  and phallos, 17-20, 24, 31
Petersen, Alice, 131
Phallic Quest, The, 82
phallic stage, 40
phallos: 9-12, 14, 16-20, 31, 35-38
  chthonic, 10, 16, 36
  concrete/symbolic, 17-20
  and individuation, 35-38
  as male god, 9-10, 35
  in psychoanalytic theory, 39-55
  solar, 10, 16, 30, 91
phallos protos, 9, 11
Phallos: Sacred Image of the Masculine, 9, 16
prenatal stage, 24-25
pre-oedipal stage, 25-28, 40-41, 43, 46
Priapus, 82

priesthood, 89
projection, 28, 53, 58-63, 65, 99, 103
psyche, 38, 55, 57, 59, 95
psychic energy, *see* libido
psychoanalytic theory, 39-55
psychoid, 10, 18-19, 116
puberty, 29-30, 65

rage, 11-14, 45, 47, 61-64, 87, 93, 98-104, 108-109
rationality, 95
Reagan, Ronald, 81, 83
receptivity, 70, 79
reductive causalism, 33, 55-56
refinement, 68-69
regression, 13, 24, 54, 64, 92
regressive restoration of persona, 65
Reis, Patricia, 22
relatedness, 69-70
religion, 18, 31, 53, 95
respect, 121-123
Restoration of the Self, The, 52
Rhea, 127
Ritter, Bruce, 110

sacrifice, 65-66, 92
sadness, 119-121
scatology, 56
Self, 18, 52-53, 59
self-object, 26, 52-53
Self-Psychology, 52-53
sensibility, 68-69
sensuality, 116-117
societal castration, 89-93
solar masculinity, 10, 16, 30, 91
son-lover syndrome, 86-87
soul, 18-19, 31, 57, 76, 124
spirit/spirituality, 17-19, 116, 125, 133
stages, of masculine development, 23-38
stereotype, 23, 66-67, 69, 119
sublimation, 13, 29, 31

suffering, 74-75, 120-121, 133
superego, 46-48, 91
Sword and the Flute, The, 107
symbiosis, 28-29, 45
symbol/symbolic, 15-20, 45, 53, 63-65, 113, 121
Symbols of Transformation, 19, 39, 57-61
synthetic analysis, 34

Tammuz, 86
teleology, 55
temenos, 119
tenderness, 73-74
"Teste Moanial," 134
thanatos, 40
Thatcher, Margaret, 85-86
timidity, 111-112
touching, 114-117
transcendence, 17, 31
transformation, masculine: 16-38, 54
    accomplishment in, 29-32
    adolescent stage, 29-30
    individuation, 32-38, 57, 59-66
    oedipal stage, 28-29

prenatal stage, 24-25
pre-oedipal stage, 25-28
of rage to anger, 99
six stages, 23-38
transgressivity, 19
Trump, Donald, 110

unconscious, 11, 54, 59, 76
uroboros, 9
urperson, 132

Valkyries, 62
virilization, 25-26
vulnerability, 70-71, 84, 116

Walküre, Die, 59
weakness, 71
Whitman, Walt, 87
wholeness, 34-38, 59
will power, 95
Wotan, 59-65
Wyly, James, 82

yin/yang, 58

Zeus, 127

Studies in Jungian Psychology by Jungian Analysts

Sewn Paperbacks

Prices and payment in $US (except in Canada, $Cdn)

The Eden Project: In Search of the Magical Other
James Hollis (Houston) ISBN 0-919123-80-5. 160 pp. $16

Jungian Psychology Unplugged: My Life As an Elephant
Daryl Sharp (Toronto) ISBN 0-919123-81-3. 160 pp. $16

The Mysterium Lectures: A Journey through Jung's *Mysterium Coniunctionis*
Edward F. Edinger (Los Angeles) ISBN 0-919123-66-X. 90 illustrations. 352 pp. $25

Conscious Femininity: Interviews with Marion Woodman
Introduction by Marion Woodman (Toronto) ISBN 0-919123-59-7. 160 pp. $16

The Middle Passage: From Misery to Meaning in Midlife
James Hollis (Houston) ISBN 0-919123-60-0. 128 pp. $16

Eros and Pathos: Shades of Love and Suffering
Aldo Carotenuto (Rome) ISBN 0-919123-39-2. 144 pp. $16

Descent to the Goddess: A Way of Initiation for Women
Sylvia Brinton Perera (New York) ISBN 0-919123-05-8. 112 pp. $16

Addiction to Perfection: The Still Unravished Bride
Marion Woodman (Toronto) ISBN 0-919123-11-2. Illustrated. 208 pp. $18pb/$25hc

The Illness That We Are: A Jungian Critique of Christianity
John P. Dourley (Ottawa) ISBN 0-919123-16-3. 128 pp. $16

Coming To Age: The Croning Years and Late-Life Transformation
Jane R. Prétat (Providence) ISBN 0-919123-63-5. 144 pp. $16

Jungian Dream Interpretation: A Handbook of Theory and Practice
James A. Hall, M.D. (Dallas) ISBN 0-919123-12-0. 128 pp. $16

Phallos: Sacred Image of the Masculine
Eugene Monick (Scranton) ISBN 0-919123-26-0. 30 illustrations. 144 pp. $16

Personality Types: Jung's Model of Typology
Daryl Sharp (Toronto) ISBN 0-919123-30-9. Diagrams. 128 pp. $16

The Sacred Prostitute: Eternal Aspect of the Feminine
Nancy Qualls-Corbett (Birmingham) ISBN 0-919123-31-7. 20 illustrations. 176 pp. $18

Close Relationships: Family, Friendship, Marriage
Eleanor Bertine (New York) ISBN 0-919123-46-5. 160 pp. $16

Swamplands of the Soul: New Life in Dismal Places
James Hollis (Houston) ISBN 0-919123-74-0. 14 illustrations. 160 pp. $16

Jung Lexicon: A Primer of Terms & Concepts
Daryl Sharp (Toronto) ISBN 0-919123-48-1. Diagrams. 160 pp. $16

Discounts: any 3-5 books, 10%; 6-9 books, 20%; 10 or more, 25%
Add Postage/Handling: 1-2 books, $3; 3-4 books, $5; 5-9 books, $10; 10 or more, free

Write or phone for **Jung at Heart** newsletter and free Catalogue of **over 90 titles**

INNER CITY BOOKS, Box 1271, Station Q, Toronto, ON M4T 2P4, Canada

Tel. (416) 927-0355 / Fax (416) 924-1814 / E-mail: sales@innercitybooks.net